CLAI

INNER BADASS

How to Live a Life of Courage and Unleash Your Personal Power

KATE MCKAY

Claim Your Inner Badass

Although the author and publisher have made every effort to ensure that the information in this book was correct at press time, the author and publisher do not assume and hereby disclaim any liability to any party for any loss, damage, or disruption caused by errors or omissions, whether such errors or omissions result from negligence, accident, or any other cause.

Adherence to all applicable laws and regulations, including international, federal, state and local governing professional licensing, business practices, advertising, and all other aspects of doing business in the US, Canada or any other jurisdiction is the sole responsibility of the reader and consumer.

Neither the author nor the publisher assumes any responsibility or liability whatsoever on behalf of the consumer or reader of this material. Any per-ceived slight of any individual or organization is purely unintentional.

The resources in this book are provided for informational purposes only and should not be used to replace the specialized training and professional judgment of a health care or mental health care professional.

Neither the author nor the publisher can be held responsible for the use of the information provided within this book. Please always consult a trained professional before making any decision regarding treatment of yourself or others.

For inquiries or bulk copies email media@kate-mckay.com.
Paperback ISBN: 978-1-7333799-0-8
Kindle ISBN:978-1-7333799-1-5
Cover and Back Photo: Amanda Ambrose
Editing: Brittany Bearden, Lillian Eagan, Caroline Laughlin

YOUR FREE GIFT!

To get the best experience with this book, download the workbook. You can grab your copy here:

http://bit.ly/Badass_Workbook

DEDICATION

(well, to YOU of course and...)

This book is dedicated to the amazing people in my life who inspire me every day to do more- to be more. I am humbled by the kindness and grace of my amazing friends, the fierce love I have for my children and my continual awe of the human spirit- how so many continue to survive and thrive and consciously choose to CLAIM their inner badass, not only despite, but because of their challenges and struggles. And so I dedicate this book to YOU, dear readers, because you believe enough in yourself to pick up this damn book. And for that I am deeply grateful.

This book is also written in loving memory to three men in my life who's feet no longer walk the earth, yet their spirit lives on through me and through all the people who loved them- my Dad, Robert McKay (who, even though he never swore in his entire life, would still appreciate this book title), my brother Matthew, who's life was taken way, way too early and then, most recently and the one hardest to accept, my boy William, who chose to leave this world on his own accord two years ago. It is Will who brought this title to life for me in a dream- a dream so real I will never forget. I love you, Buddy.

Tell me, what is it you plan to do

With your one wild and precious life?

— MARY OLIVER

(excerpt from the poem The Summer Day)

Unspoken Axiom for Being a Badass*

1. If you are a badass, you don't have to tell people you are one. You just are.
2. Badasses spot other badasses in the crowd. They are the ones helping the old lady up over the curb, pushing someone's broken car off the road, working tirelessly behind the scenes on something they believe in, chilling out holding space for others.
3. A badass knows who they are. They have been through challenges, been knocked down and have stood back up, brushed off and moved on ahead.
4. A badass won't engage in conflicts that are pointless, disrespectful or unnecessary. They know it's not only foolish, but a waste of time.
5. A badass is confident, not cocky. They have nothing to prove or defend, especially against the haters.
6. Badass people are kind, yet resolute when it comes to their principles and values.
7. Badasses spend quality time fostering the growth of others. They understand the high value of quality relationships.
8. Badasses won't do dumb shit just to get attention or accolades.
9. Badasses can usually pinpoint the time in their lives when they gained badass status.
10. A badass isn't afraid to speak their truth, say they are sorry, or be the first one to reach out and call a truce when necessary. They hold the high watch; people trust them, and are grateful that they are on their side.

*A partial list, readers please feel free to add your own on the Facebook page (Claim Your Inner Badass)

And so, this is the part where you decide it's time to claim your inner badass…

TABLE OF CONTENTS

INTRODUCTION: THE AUTHOR'S JOURNEY TO CLAIM HER BADASS

Has there been a time in your life when you remember feeling truly badass?

I distinctly remember the first time I felt this way. I was 20 years old, attending Bennington College in Vermont. There was no gym at the school, so myself and a couple other students pulled together a makeshift workout area behind the mailroom. I was always a super-hyper kid, a total spaz. What I discovered was that lifting weights tapped into me somehow; something about the weight of the bar and the pressing soothed me and righted my racing mind. Suddenly, all things went still, and I remember sitting up and saying to myself, wow, I like this. And for what felt like the first time in my life, all things went still and I felt an overwhelming sense of peace.

Thirty years later, moving my body through exercise, in whatever form, still sets me straight. It makes me feel grounded, peaceful, and alive. And yah, badass.

This sense of inner awareness and hyper-flow has been a fundamental aspect of my life— from the greatest highs to the greatest lows. In order to conquer anything in my life, I must begin with feeling grounded in my body.

This hyper-flow is how I survived growing up in a family of eleven, the tragic murder of my brother Matthew, my chaotic and financially imperiled marriage that ended in divorce, raising three out-of-the-box children, a successful career as an athlete, my entrepreneurial success growing a multi-million dollar company, and most recently, the loss of my son Will by suicide in 2017.

The consistency in all of this insanity, both wonderful and tragic, was that I always knew where my sanctuary was. It wasn't some fleeting thing outside of me, floating through the clouds in some ADHD haze (yes, I am a certified and proud member of the club) or buried in some hole in the backyard, or in some crappy relationships, or in another dead-end job.

Nope. It was within me. I call it God. You can call it what you want. Inner knowing, your gut, divine guidance, Jesus, Allah, Buddha. Even Nothingness. Your spiritual truth is all your own, and I honor and respect that. There are many paths to peace and knowing. Something I find a great relief, not a conflict.

Growing up in a big family, while most of my siblings were drugging and drinking, I was doing cartwheels in the lawn and spinning around on my bike. Our home was full of laughter, music, pot smoke and tension. When I heard the news that my brother was murdered, I retreated to my sanctuary, the only place where I felt my greatest sense of peace— the gym. The day after the memorial service my Dad, my fitness mentor, and I ran a road race in an attempt to find solace and connection.

When I grew my multi-million-dollar business as a single mom with three kids, I simultaneously competed as a bikini and fitness competitor from the age of 43 to 55. When my son took his own life, I was training a client in the gym. In the following months, I hiked some of the 4,000-footers in New Hampshire's White Mountains in his memory.

Was I running? Hell no. What I was doing was rebuilding my reserves, processing my success, grief, fear, losses, and having a big ole' one-on-one conference call with God. It was only after my own "40 days in the wilderness" that I was able to come back to my life more clear, more positive, and more powerful than ever.

The greatest successful people out there share this belief, from Tony Robbins to Oprah, being connected to your body is a crucial part of your success story. My number one goal in life is to share this sense of peace and personal power with others. It's why God put me here— to help others heal their suffering and help them develop the tools to embrace a more prosperous and kick-ass life.

Through coaching, training, speaking, writing, from kids, to people taking their last breath, to those most wealthy, to the most destitute, with every race, religion, and sexual orientation, I see people's brilliance, even when they don't see it. I serve as a powerful mirror to others' greatness, because I have been to the precipice. Because I have stood alone in the storm. Because I wasn't afraid to dig deep. Because I knew I was, and remain, undaunted.

Some of the following essays, articles, and interactives are a compilation of excerpts I have written for *The Newburyport Daily News*. Others are excerpts from my book *Living Sexy Fit at Any Age*. Still others are from journals, originals, and scraps of notes I uncovered as I put together this book. Writing is an ever-evolving birthing process of new and hashed over ideas. This book is all about that.

In the following pages I will share my winning strategies— the strategies that have been the secret sauce for hundreds of my clients and including myself to become badasses in all areas of our lives.

I look forward to taking this journey with you. If one article, one sentence, one word, elicits a spark of recognition or seed of inspiration in you, I have done my job as a writer. I thank you for the opportunity to accompany you on your own amazing journey to badassery.

First, before we launch into the meat of the matter, I would like to say to all of you out there as your Badass Coach:

That you deserve to be heard.

That your thoughts and feelings are worthy of expression.

That your body is your own to celebrate and to powerfully live through.

That no one is the boss of you but you.

That playing small is bullshit.

That your body is your vessel to which your brilliance is birthed. Treat it like a temple. Work it like a beast.

That I believe in you.

That you matter.

Yes, you.

Okay, so let's begin…

Living Powerfully: Five Action STEPS in Claiming Your Badassery

"Low self-confidence isn't a life sentence. Self-confidence can be learned, practiced, and mastered—just like any other skill. Once you master it, everything in your life will change for the better." — Barrie Davenport

1. Get Real— Facing and Naming the Elephant in the Room
2. Let Go— Release what No Longer Serves You
3. Fueling Your Inner Badass
4. Finding Your Beast Mode— Small Steps for Big Wins
5. Celebrate Yourself— Confidence from the Inside Out

As a coach, entrepreneur, speaker, writer and author, I totally get that life's challenges and being in a perpetual state of overwhelm can literally knock us to our knees. This often-grueling process of just getting through the day is REAL, and it can weigh us down not only physically, but emotionally and spiritually as well.

I think back on a time in my life several years ago when my self-doubt and self-loathing reached critical mass, a time when my body no longer felt like my own and my life seemed unmanageable. It was like an alien had taken residence in my mind. I felt confused, weepy, raging, and giddy all at once.

Okay, I was a hot mess.

I had just given birth to my third child, financial pressure and emotional distance was building in my marriage, and I felt the walls crumbling down around me.

I remember one day in particular as if it was yesterday: I dragged myself into the gym, hoping and praying that it would be the day that would rekindle that long lost feeling of being unstoppable—the same feeling I uncovered in my makeshift mail-room gym at age 20. Since that first day grinding the weights, the gym became my safe haven— the place where I reclaimed my super-power.

What I saw that day startled me; the image of myself in the gym mirror—I looked like a big, swollen tick full of misery. I was unrecognizable to myself. The look in my eyes was that of utter defeat and desperation.

At that point, taking immediate action became completely and absolutely non-negotiable. It was an all-time low, and I knew that I needed to rescue myself, because no one was going to do it for me.

Can you relate to this story? Have you experienced anything like this? The proverbial dark night of the soul?

Or are you experiencing something similar now as you look at yourself in the mirror and feel this crazy incongruity of knowing that the person looking back at you is by no way a true reflection of who you are.

Are you hungry and disturbed enough by your own reflection to start doing what you have to do to release fear and self-loathing, shame and self-doubt, or whatever emotion is keeping you from living the life you truly in your heart desires?

Are you ready to begin the process of embracing a new, more confident you?

Are you ready to become a badass?

Are you ready to take IMMEDIATE and RADICAL action to get your ship righted?

I wrote this book because my biggest desire in life is to inspire YOU to take action to live the life of a champion.

Beginning Your Badass Journey

"Trust yourself. Create the kind of self that you will be happy to live with all your life. Make the most of yourself by fanning the tiny, inner sparks of possibility into flames of achievement." — Golda Meir

Let's dig deeper into the process of becoming a badass so you have the tools you need to get real, get radical, and rebirth the healthiest and most authentic version of yourself.

1. Get Real: Facing and Naming the Elephant in the Room

Our resistance to face the music of our past is often the real cause as to why diet and exercise plans fail, or other life goals and dreams get left by the wayside. In fact, in any area of your life where you are feeling like you are losing it is usually a direct result of some unhealed trauma that's been stuffed away, ignored.

Unfortunately, those traumas fester in your body and start rearing their ugly heads at the most inopportune time. For example: your approaching wedding day following a parent's death, a financial loss, or. This is a huge part of my coaching work with clients. I often find their greatest truth, their badass, lies on the other side of their unresolved trauma.

- Made to feel less than and ashamed? Your body remembers.
- Called fat and ridiculed? That memory is still lodged.
- Pushed around by someone and still feeling the bruises?

- Crushed in a love relationship? Yup, your body stored that as well.

Your body stores old memories like a bulletproof vault, whether we remember them consciously or not. I don't mean to be a downer, but this is the God's honest truth.

(Below I have provided space for you to share your thoughts; however, if you would prefer to write elsewhere visit http://bit.ly/CYIB_Workbook to access the virtual workbook)

Workbook #1:

Please describe a time when you were made to feel small and not valued as a person.

____

____

____

____

____

How do we cope? We use alcohol, food, sex, and other addictive things to stuff those memories down and away so we don't have to deal. As Dr. Phil asks, with his dead-pan expression, layered in irony and wit,

"How is that working for you?!"

Yah, I know, not so well. And, I am sorry for that. And you're definitely not alone.

So, are you ready to take action? Are you ready to release, let go, so that you can embrace that inner badass and live the life you want and, most importantly, deserve?

I am personally committed to ensuring that this happens for you, so let's move on to the next step in your transformation.

But, before we do so, please know this: any nasty thing that was spoken to you or any yucky way people made you feel was their issue, NOT YOURS! The quicker you get that, the sooner you will feel more aligned with who you came here to be, and you will become unstoppable.

Workbook #2:

1. Please journal below on what you really want. I mean *really* want, with a burning in your belly that you may even be embarrassed to say out loud. It's time to say it out loud and put it down on paper.

____

____

____

____

____

2. What do you need to get what you want out of life? Speaking your needs is tough for a lot of people, but you have to figure that out and name it, so you can attain greater success and satisfaction in your life.

3. What are you committed to? There is a big difference between just being interested in something and being completely committed. I don't do just "interested", for the record. Do you want a good life or a great one? Thought so. Write what you are committed to in your journey to greatness below.

4. Okay, so why are you committed to your best self? You have to be clear on your *why*, because from this answer comes the motivation and the action to live your best life. Remember this is YOUR *why*, not someone else's! Go ahead and write. Please do not skip over this.

5. Are you ready to take immediate action to regain your sense of inner personal power and positive self-esteem?

6. Why? Yup, that question again! Write it down!

___

___

2. Let Go: Release What No Longer Serves You

It may seem counterintuitive, but in order to transform, we need to start at "what needs to go" to live a life of greatness. In fact, the number one roadblock I see with my clients is patterns of self-sabotage and self-doubt that cripple their ability to live in alignment with who they truly are and who they came here to be.

Whether my client hires me because they want to lose weight, find a great relationship, start their own company or write a book, we often need to start by replaying stories that are on rewind and repeat in their head.

Are you ready to release behaviors that no longer serve you? It starts with reframing the stories of your past by releasing self-sabotaging language, thoughts, and behaviors.

TOLERATIONS

A great way to do this is to make a list of things you are tolerating in your life and start eliminating these things from the list.

What are you tolerating in your life that has to go? People, places, things, behaviors? First you name it, then you have to deal with it.

Benefits of having tolerations resolved:

- Less stress.
- Increased productivity.
- Easier relationships.

- Healthier boundaries.
- Increased self-esteem and self-worth.
- More sex (sure, why not?).

Need some suggestions of some tolerations? Happy to oblige!

50+ Tolerations:

- Not enough storage space for all my office files.
- Not staying committed to my workout goals.
- A desk full of stacks of stuff.
- Peeling wallpaper, chipped paint.
- A partner who is not kind to my child or children.
- Being overweight.
- A web page that needs updating.
- A dated hairstyle.
- A guest bedroom that needs cleaning up (it looks like a storage room).
- Not enough time scheduled for dreaming.
- Not enough time spent in the garden.
- Not setting time aside to meditate.
- Not saving money every month.
- Not getting paid enough for my work.
- Clients who cancel appointments at the last moment.
- Excessive clutter.
- Investments that should be reevaluated but haven't been.
- House walls that need patching.
- Not having a spare key for the car.
- Unfinished home improvement projects.
- Mortgage and car payments are out of my comfort zone.
- Negative attitudes of people at my work.

- Poor customer service and inadequate responses from vendors.
- Eating too much sugar and salt.
- Low levels of reserves.
- Too many possessions that need to be cleaned.
- Drinking too much.
- A constant need for home maintenance and repairs.
- My lack of creative outlet.
- Being part of a profession where I can no longer relate to the goals and standards.
- Knowing all my debt will not be paid off when I retire or have a baby.
- Inadequate retirement fund.
- Demands on my time by my children.
- A former spouse who does not contribute time or money to raising our children.
- Mildew on the plastic shower curtain.
- Spiderwebs in the corners.
- A dining room table currently covered with stuff not related to dining.
- Someone close to you with an undiscussed drug or alcohol problem.
- Gross towels.
- Going to the doctor.
- Electronics and wires that you don't know what they go to.
- Not knowing where your money is going.
- Dirty refrigerator.
- Not getting your intimate needs met with your partner.
- Unorganized tools.
- Dirty windows.

- Unresolved grief.
- Dishes and pots and pans that are not to your liking.
- Underwear that no longer fits.
- Not enough hugs.
- Burned out lightbulbs.
- Excess stuff in your trunk.
- Socks with holes.
- Being ghosted again.
- Ugly shoes.
- A bad kisser.
- Under sink mess.

Mark the tolerations that resonate with you, add your own, then start checking them off the list one by one. Be consistent and attack these tolerations like a beast.

This exercise is a gamechanger for my clients, and I bet the same will apply to you. The freedom when you handle your tolerations is immense. I had one client who, by handling her tolerations, increased her revenue by 40%. Another client lost 40 pounds when he eliminated his top three tolerations. You can have these wonderful results too!

Workbook #3:

Write yours down here:

1.

____

2.

____

3.

4.

5.

6.

7.

8.

9.

10.

Start crossing off tolerations from your list today. Join the Facebook page (Claim Your Inner Badass) and share your wins. We love to read your success stories!

3. Fueling Your Inner Badass

So why do so many of us experience epic fails on achieving our wants and dreams in life? One word: FEAR. Fear of failure. Fear of success. Fear of letting go. Fear of judgment. Fear of YOU-NAME-IT.

Our fear and resistance to face the previously stated "music of our past" is often a catalyst to failing diet or exercise regimes, business plans gone awry, and relationships falling apart. Our commitment falls away when our "ugly" reveals its head.

But I am here to tell you that you are ready. I know you are, or you wouldn't have read this far with a burning in the belly to say yes. Yes to *me*, yes to *you*, and a big HELL YES to taking the plunge.

Let's keep moving into action so that you can embrace that inner badass that is ready for battle.

This is worth repeating:

Please remember any nasty thing that was spoken to you or the yucky way people made you feel was their issue, NOT YOURS! The expression that people didn't know better is crap. It is our personal responsibility to heal our stuff, not pass it on to future generations. That means it becomes paramount that we do our personal work, so we can be fully in our power.

Having healthy boundaries and feeling all warm on the inside is the best and sweetest revenge. And once you acknowledge this crazy-ass truth, you no longer have to play small games with the cheaters and liars. There is no turning back, because you have become... unstoppable.

Workbook #4

1. Pick any area of your life where you are ready for a change-up (body image, finances, relationships, you name it). What behaviors, actions, even people are hindering your success in this area?

2. What self-sabotaging behavior are you ready to let go of? Write them down here. By naming them, we give them light, so we can love on those parts of ourselves that need care and attention. Often, once we name out loud the things, we have shame around, we free ourselves from our emotional bondage. (Check out Brene Brown's work if you haven't already. Her book, *Daring Greatly*, is a real eye-opening experience)

3. Please write below a couple small micro-habits that you now embrace that will allow you to unleash your inner warrior! You got this.

Micro-habit (n)- *a small change you can adopt, that you can hook on to another action in your day. Make them small and doable. Success starts with small steps.*

____

____

____

____

____

Remember, this journey is a slow slog, not a race. Be gentle, yet consistent in your process. You deserve that level of tender care. You really do.

4. Finding Your Beast Mode: Small Steps for Big Wins

Due to the fact that I am both an athlete and a coach, I am particularly fond of sports metaphors, so I love the term "beast mode".

Even though that expression has an aggressive ring to it, I find the basic tenet of the phrase applicable to anyone striving to feel more fulfilled in their life.

When I Googled the term, the first definition that came up was this: **Beast mode** (n) a state of performing something, especially difficult activities, with extreme power, skill, or determination. Oh, I really like that! This is a perfect example of what it feels like to be in the zone of badassery (yah, I make stuff up).

So, in order to begin your own self-defined beast mode journey, it is important that you find a way to tap into your body's energy source— this will bring you closer to ways in which you can feel the most connected and powerful within yourself.

Once you find a way to tap into this energy circuit, you will experience a turbo boost of success in all areas of your life.

And as the saying goes, all you need to have is a mustard seed of faith to begin. Do you have that? Even a grain of hope? I sure do hope so.

As far as what modality to choose, no one can decide this for you. I personally love how it feels to lift weights. Why? Because it calms my crazy ADHD mind down. To me, the gym is a sanctuary. It allows me to embody the flow state, which I am able to channel successfully in multiple areas of my life.

It doesn't matter what you choose. I have clients who tap into all different types of movement modalities including fencing, ballroom dancing and hiking. It doesn't matter what it is as long as you are doing something that gets your heart pumping and your endorphins flowing.

Let's do some reflecting together. What are some ways that you enjoyed moving your body as a child? Perhaps when you felt most free and synchronized in your body, mind, and spirit. I understand that not everyone has an athletic mindset. Personally, I didn't learn how to harness this in myself until I was in my early twenties. One of my recent clients just tapped in and hit her stride at age 68 and she's rocking it! It's never too late!

You must be committed to tapping into your inner Olympian, your primal human desire to propel yourself, to move this magical machine you were born into. Are you ready?

(Can you tell this stuff actually excites me? ;-))

Let's move on to some questions:

Workbook #5:

1. What did you love to do as a child, at age 5?

At age 12?

At age 25?

2. Thinking back on your childhood, what did you love to do for activities?

3. Did it take place inside or outside?

4. With one other person, a group, or solo?

5. Are you more of a morning or night person?

6. What do you remember giving you joy?

7. Where do you remember feeling the most safe and peaceful as a child? Why? This is important because often times tapping into our peace is a gateway into our badassery.

____

____

____

____

____

Great job.

Now, we want to translate those emotional memories into creating a movement plan that you will not only be able to commit to, but enjoy. Finding the right movement plan to fit your lifestyle is key to getting and keeping your fit mojo. Part of becoming a badass means living in your power and joy from the inside out.

List of possible exercise modalities:

- Walking
- Running
- Biking
- Rolling skating
- Treadmill
- Weightlifting
- Yoga
- Stretching
- Dancing in your kitchen
- Climbing stairs

- Group Classes
- Zumba
- Line dancing
- Aerobics
- Slow flow yoga
- CrossFit
- Spin classes
- Pole dancing
- Pilates
- Ballroom Dancing
- Martial Arts
- Competitive team sports
- Basketball
- Soccer
- Running clubs
- Tennis

Phew! That's a whole lot of action!

Let's chill out for a few and talk about one of my favorite, and crucially important, topics to embrace on your badass journey…

Restoration

Ahh, the delicious concept of *restoration.* I LOVE this word. Knowing how to chill the "f" out is a crucial part of how to remain in the badass zone— especially when life, people, places, and things are on red alert around you. I like to crown myself "Queen of the Chill" when life gets particularly harried. I consider it one of my superpowers and I preach this endlessly to my clients.

We have nothing to prove acting like we need to do more, say more, spend more, lift more, or be more than anyone else. When you are unstoppable, others' opinions of you become insignificant. When you are aligned with your higher purpose, you tend to treat people in your life with more kindness and understanding. When you are effortlessly adjusting your boundaries to the flow and energies around you, you no longer need to manage how people perceive you.

How does that sound? Pretty darn good, right?

So, ask yourself these questions to get this flow going...

Workbook #6:

1. What are some ways I can restore my inner balance and be more in flow with the energies around me?

____

____

____

____

____

2. What are the habits I can implement right now to have more peace and acceptance in my life?

____

____

3. How can I tap into more of these "chill feelings": throughout my day, especially when I am feeling harried, raging, and out of sorts?

Again, focusing on micro-shifts is what helps the most successful people make the biggest gains in their lives. Please set your parameters to best help restore your inner flow.

Those who are on their badass journey know how to rest. Set yourself up to live your best A-game by doing the same.

5. Celebrate Yourself: Confidence from the Inside Out.

NEWS FLASH: The process of moving into your greatness is wonderful, amazing, and often a little scary too! Be prepared for all of it!

What is standing in your way? Be honest with yourself. What changes are you ready to take on, because if you have read this far, there is a piece of you that is ready to roll.

Workbook #7:

Below is a great tool to get your badass show on the road. My clients use this exercise when they are stuck in a logjam and need clarity to push through limited thinking. It's a game-changer. Try it out and share your ah-ha's on the Facebook Group (Claim Your Inner Badass).

Replacing the "BUT" with the "AND" The Power of Your Language Made Manifest

Switch one word, switch your whole life!

List three areas you've wanted to make changes in (ie. lose weight, find a great relationship, make way more money, have a greater connection with God/Peace/Joy). Be sure to frame it in a positive.

Examples from Clients:

> I would like to lose 10 pounds. I would like to switch jobs. I want a great relationship.

1.____

2.____

3.____

Complete the sentences using your answers above.

Examples from Clients:

I would lose 10 pounds but I don't have time. I would switch jobs but I am not sure if I will make enough money. I want a great relationship but there are so many losers out there. I would have a spiritual practice but I don't know how to go about it.

1. I would ____________________, but ____________________

2. I would ____________________, but ____________________

3. I would ____________________, but ____________________

Now make the one-word change. (Make sure your sentence is action-based.)

Examples from Clients:

I will lose 10 pounds and I will begin today to exercise 30 minutes a day and cut out all chips. (true story) I will switch jobs and will follow my passion to help the homeless and will hire a coach to help strategize this transition. I will commit to a daily spiritual practice by meditating 10 minutes each day and have more peace and joy in my life.

Your turn, badass:

1. I will ________________________and____________________

2. I will ________________________and____________________

3. I will ________________________and____________________

Please share your ah-ha's! We want to support you on your badass transformation!

When I first completed this exercise I up-leveled my life and moved into my "BIG". The part that scared me the most was not knowing WHO I was going to be if I wasn't my self-loathing and self-doubt!

Who knew that my biggest fear, my dysfunction, my modus operandi was keeping my inner badass on the back burner of life?

We were all put on this beautiful planet— in this abundant world— for a reason. Each of us is unique; it is our darn job to define our purpose and live it like a boss, wouldn't you agree?

Why is it that we spend so much time letting others define our lives for us? Are you one of those people? Are you waiting for someone else to tell you to turn left or turn right? Are you finally ready to take hold of your own GPS and put your life on overdrive?

Yay, I thought so!

The cool part of this badass journey is that this whole transformational process starts within. This allows us to discover our life purpose, live in abundance, revel in self-love and acceptance, and serve at our highest level doing our greatest good. We cannot live this way if we are letting someone else write the agenda or steer the ship of our lives.

What stories do you want to be telling some day from your rocking chair? Please make them juicy, exciting, and uniquely yours.

To live your life in celebration requires some daily action steps, so that you are never too far off your fit-and-fab bullseye. Sure, crappy things happen. Tragedy can strike our lives and and knock us to our knees; however, if you develop your resiliency muscle, and keep self-love and acceptance at the core of how you live, you will be amazed at how your life begins to look and feel.

I want that for you. Joy, peace and an inner confidence that keeps your life roaring with passion and desire. This is possible when you commit to daily actions to live your best and most kick-ass life.

Workbook #8:

Action Plan to Keep the Celebration Going

Put a pen to paper and write down IN DETAIL your vision for yourself, including what you will be doing, who you will be with, what the weather is like, how you are feeling, etc.... LIVE THIS EXPERIENCE IN YOUR BODY, MIND and SOUL!

1 month

____

____

3 months

____

____

6 months

____

____

12 months

____

____

Create your Support Team

Who is going to hold you to your highest and best, even when you don't feel like it (because sometimes you just won't)— TRUST ME, I get this one! That is exactly why I have a business coach, fitness coach, therapist, and even an astrologer to keep me on the straight and narrow. It takes a village, people!

They have witnessed me in my "ugly" and they love on me anyway. Why? Because they truly see my most authentic and best self, even when I don't see it. And honestly, there is something weird about the fact that I feel an obligation to not let them down. I mean heck, if they think I am pretty awesome, maybe I have to go with my mustard seed of faith that I am possibly as cool as they think I am.

I firmly believe that the most successful people understand they need a team to help them reach their A-game. I certainly couldn't be coaching A-game clients without expecting the same for myself.

Who is holding you up to your highest level of yourself? If you don't have that person, maybe it's time to start looking.

Workbook #9:

1. List one to three people who you will share your dreams with and who will make sure you are staying in your A-Game mentality, NO EXCUSES! (P.S. you won't always like them, but will ALWAYS love them! ☺)

____

____

____

2. How often will I check in with them?

____

____

____

3. How would I like them to hold me accountable? Be specific.

____

____

____

____

____

____

Great work. Let's keep going...

YOU ARE THE LIFE OF THE PARTY, LIVE IT!

"If you're serious about changing your life, you'll find a way. If you're not, you'll find an excuse." —Jen Sincero

Be prepared to have people be drawn to you that normally wouldn't even have said "hello" to you. Confident people attract all kinds of attention.

You see, when you are at peace and love yourself for who you are, just by doing your thing and being unconcerned about what others think or being crushed by your own self-judgement, you SHINE— plain and simple.

This is not about ego.

This is not about being phony.

And this is not about being full of yourself.

This is about living in your true and authentic self. Because when we celebrate ourselves— our uniqueness, our strengths, our beauty in and out— the world around us begins to reflect our own inner-greatness.

By celebrating yourself and taking small steps to feel strong and powerful from within, you are serving as a role model to others— your kids, your friends, your intimate partner— for what AUTHENTICITY and INTEGRITY look and feel like.

Be your most amazing and authentic self and carry your inner celebration with you wherever you go.

With a sparkle in your eye and knowing that you are so completely and totally worth it, I celebrate YOU!

"Success is doing what you want, when you want, where you want, with whom you want, as much as you want." — Tony Robbins

Umm, yes, please…

There's Gotta Be an Easier Way (and Other Crap You Tell Yourself)

"When you are truly genuine, there will inevitably be people who do not accept you. And in that case, you must be your own badass self." —*Katie Goodman*

The first question people ask someone who has lost weight, found a new love, or landed a great job is, "How did you do it?" What they really want to know is whether that person has discovered a new and pain-free way to getting fit, attractive, or rich. Was it a pill? A special diet? A website? A plastic surgeon? Some other get-rich-quick scheme?

And when they find out that the key to success was just clean eating and exercise, or healing yourself completely before getting out there in the dating world, or hiring someone to spiff up your résumé, they are disappointed and think dejectedly, *That will never be me. I could never do that.*

And so I ask, why not? Why can't that be you? Why is it that so many of us resign to a less-than-optimal lifestyle? And more importantly, what is it that motivates the people who have succeeded in undergoing such a lifestyle transformation to live powerfully and tap into their inner greatness?

When I ask people who have nailed their fitness and lifestyle goals what motivated them to take the plunge and make the necessary changes to live their lives to the fullest, they often describe a gradual, internal shift that expanded the sense of possibility in themselves. Then one day, *boom*, they felt the shift. They felt they reached a new state of being— more confident, less stressed and less anxious in all areas of their lives.

Wouldn't it be great if we could "just do it", as Nike proclaims? Why is it that some people are able to push through resistance to be their best where others fail to tread?

Understanding what motivates people to transform their lives oftentimes precludes the "just do it" mentality. People are motivated by all kinds of things: looking more attractive, fitting in their wedding dress, impressing their peers, proving to family that they have the willpower to succeed, etc. What do all these things have in common? These are all extrinsic or external motivators that affect how other people perceive us. And guess what? These external motivators are much less likely to stick, because it is not enough to make the shift for someone else—we need to want it for ourselves from within ourselves.

Unstoppability doesn't come from wanting to do all this work for someone else; it comes from YOU wanting it bad enough that you are going to attain it, whatever the cost in effort, exertion, or resources. Sure, you can be driven to get fit to spite someone—someone calls you fat, your kid pokes at you, your partner eye rolls at you when you go for more dessert— but none of these episodes are going to help you make lasting change. You really have to want to do it for you.

Intrinsic or internal motivators are driven by our desire to live more in line with our own values, the essential nature of who we are. When you are out of alignment, you feel it. Things hurt, your mood is off, you just don't feel yourself. Getting clear on what you really want, not what others want, is the name of the game for long-lasting and positive change.

With clients, I continually talk about their evolving personal vision–what drives them on a daily basis to be their best selves. The process is definitely not always a pretty one (getting fit, finding love, and seeking meaningful work is sweaty and grueling, mentally and physically). But the rewards are huge on all levels when they attain their goals from the inside out.

What about you? What is it that you want for yourself? How will your life be different when you are living your life more in line with your own values? When you are feeling your best and brightest self? Who are you with? What are you doing? What season is it? What are you wearing? The more you can fill in the blanks, the clearer the vision, the closer you will be to living the life you deserve.

There is no magic bullet to transforming your life. This process is not for the faint of heart. However, spending a few moments to think of what internally motivates you to embrace positive change will be worth its weight in gold. Give yourself permission to let go and really experience how it will feel to let that badass you have jammed up inside, be free.

Let today be the day you start to move towards a bigger and better version of you. Embrace the feeling of what it will be like to have a body that moves through space with power and vitality; with a mind that is clearer and more focused, and a heart that is fierce. Share your hopes and dreams with someone that will support you on your journey, and most importantly, raise the badass flag, and enjoy the ride!

Workbook #10:

1. How will your life be different when you are living your life on your terms?

2. How will you feel when you achieve your goals?

3. Who are you with?

4. What are you doing?

5. How are people describing you?

6. What do you need right now?

It's all pretty exciting and a tad scary, isn't it? Honestly, if you are not afraid, your dream is not big enough. You can do it. Your time is now.

Getting Clear — Creating Healthy Relationships with Yourself and Others

"What the heck is happening?": Understanding Your Emotions through Transformation

"Talk to yourself like you would to someone you love." —Brene Brown

As you move into your badass self, you will experience some emotions that are best addressed at the outset, such as:

1. Unexplained emotional fogginess.
2. Clarity of ideas that shock you.
3. Intolerance of people lying and not being straight-shooters.
4. Hurt feelings that seem out-of-context with the given situation.
5. Moments of bliss you just can't explain.
6. Uncontrollable laughter.
7. Uncontrollable tears.
8. Peace.
9. Joy.
10. Relief.

You just start feeling different...

Like really different.

And you can't quite put your finger on what it is.

People around you notice it, too, and are not quite sure what has happened either. Where is the "old" you?

Congratulations! You are moving into a transformational period where your old ways of being no longer serve you, and your greater calling— the Bigger and Better YOU— is waiting to be born.

Welcome home, Badass.

This is the moment you have been waiting for. So why does it feel so… strange?

As your coach, I am here to help you, support you, and challenge you through this crazy stage as you set out to live your breakthrough life. You are going to be fine. More than fine – you are going to be amazing.

Let's go over some strategies you can use to make this process easier, not just for you, but those who surround you as well. We will talk more about these rollercoaster emotions that are often experienced in the process of transformation.

First, even though certain reactions you experience may seem out of context, know that sometimes, if a particular issue is laden with emotional wounds that have not been addressed, you may unknowingly react completely out-of-context to the actual event at hand. Be forewarned.

For example:

Your spouse is late without calling, and shows up just after you have put dinner on the table. You flip out.

or:

Your kids don't say thank you. Again. You seethe.

Reactions? Normal. Why is that, you may ask?

What is happening is that old wounds are surfacing, so it's important to resolve them once and for all. If tardiness or not getting a say in something truly matters, then you are being faced with a great opportunity to clear that up head-on so you can live in a new level of integrity and clarity.

Make sense?

This is called ***creating healthy boundaries*** and maintaining a higher level of self-care. This is about being clear on what is acceptable to you, without judgment of others, so you are more aligned with your authentic self. Bravo!

Will there be bumps on the way? Sure.

Will you need to say you're sorry a few times? Perhaps.

Will others become more clear on what is important to you and why? Absolutely.

Congratulations for putting your integrity of self at the center of your transformation. It takes some work, but the steps you take here and now are not only invaluable, they are essential for your growth.

Again, understand that adapting new ways of being and communicating, stirs up some real juicy stuff. It surfaces now with such power and intensity; it is a reminder of what you must release to be finally free of your past. And this, my friend, is way good. You cannot transform without it.

To be clear: when you are in the midst of it, it won't feel all good. Not even a drop sometimes. But soon, the clarity and release you experience will be so worth it. I promise. I have worked with hundreds of people who have been challenged through this journey. You will make it through as well, more powerful and focused than ever.

You will also find that as you move into a higher level of integrity, your goals become more attainable. You feel a greater sense of peace, and you may also experience an increased sense of abundance. Your relationships are richer. Success occurs with less effort and more ease.

Now, doesn't that sound like it will so be worth it???

Important Self-Care Tip: Talk through issues with your coach, therapist, or accountability partner. Write in a journal or meditate, but do not give up on your dream of living an amazing breakthrough life.

Yes, it will require work and effort and some uncomfortable moments, but it is totally worth it!

Often, quitters are more concerned with how far they have to go than how far they have come. That is not YOU. <u>You</u> are not a quitter!

Stay clear on your goals, choose action over reaction, and stay in self-love and self-acceptance. Picture how you want conversations to end up and hold steady on that vision. Be less worried about being right. Be most concerned with staying in your integrity and in your grace.

Workbook #11:

Please review the eliciting questions below. Some answers may surprise you as you read what you wrote. Be kind in your reactions, as emotions can come up that have been latent for much time (days, weeks, maybe years). And, once again, please seek a licensed therapist if you are having a particularly challenging time working through past traumas. Nothing will speed you along faster than healing old wounds so you are free to live more fully in the present. You deserve that freedom starting today.

As you think about your transformation, ask yourself the following:

1. What are some things that could get in the way of achieving my goals and living a kick-ass life?

____

____

____

____

____

2. Are there people I think may not support my transformation?

____

____

____

3. Why?

4. What conversations will be necessary in order for me to feel supported?

5. Are there people in my life I may have to temporarily or permanently let go?

6. Ask yourself this: if I do not attain my goals and dreams, what do I lose? Am I willing to take that risk?

7. What do I need *right now* to become a badass?

Tidbits from Kate:

Want to increase your Happiness Quotient?

Give a little sugar to the three nuggets below:

1. Appreciation: digging what you have, seeing what it is. Just like a big hug, appreciation asks for nothing and gives everything. Try it.
2. Personal Power: taking responsibility for what is yours and taking action on living a JUICY life. Responsibility by action. It's super sexy.
3. Leading with Your Strength: What makes your heart skip when you do it? What did you love when you were five years old? What do people keep telling you you're really good at? Okay, now go ahead and do more of it. Building up your weaknesses while diminishing your strengths is so old school.

Want to really boost your personal strength knowledge times ten? Buy the book or purchase a code online for *Strengths Finder 2.0*, take the test, and be prepared to be awed by the many ways you rock. You will discover your top five strengths. This test changed my life, really! Check it out.

Celebrate each and every small change you make. The first step to being a badass is accepting the fact that no one is going to want you to win like you do. Be your own champion. It's your time to claim it.

The Positive Approach to Being a Badass By Using the Power of Vision Creation

"Whatever you hold in your mind on a consistent basis is exactly what you will experience in your life." —Tony Robbins

Creating a powerful vision for yourself is paramount when planning to be a badass. Without a vision or a profound sense of hope for the future, you will forever feel stuck in the proverbial boat without a paddle. You deserve more.

It's important to step back from the pace of life and carve out a time where you can allow yourself to dream, to ponder, to reflect on how you want your life to move forward. You have a choice: to either steer your own sled or be dragged.

Let's get into ways you can live fully in your amazing life.

Are you ready…?

- To feel more energetic and vibrant, with less worry and stress?
- To stop beating yourself up over not succeeding in your health and wellness goals?
- To start focusing your energy on what works and how you want your life to be better, to not only look better, but to feel better all around?
- To no longer settle for unsupportive people that sabotage your hopes and dreams?

- To claim your own personal power and live with more courage and vitality?

If the answer is yes, great. Let's start by applying the latest research on behavioral change, so we can attain the desired lifestyle change-up pronto.

What is being shown in recent studies (Bayramoglu and Sahin, 2015) is that change is most likely to be long-lasting through a positive and forward-looking environment, versus an environment of negativity and self-flagellation.

Surprised? Based on my work with hundreds of clients, I am not surprised at all. In fact, I am thrilled these studies confirm my core belief— that in order for us to make lasting and positive change, we must start with a loving and centered growth mindset versus a negative, fixed mindset (Mindset, Carol Dweck, PhD 2006).

The good news is the field of positive psychology uses the scientific method to focus not on the pathology of our current condition, like many other branches of psychology, but rather on altering our thoughts and core beliefs to affect behavioral change. This research makes coaches like me very happy!

Martin Seligman, MD, considered to be the father of Positive Psychology, defines optimal living as the intersection where contentment and satisfaction (of one's past) converge with hope and optimism (for the future), allowing us to live more fully in the present.

In other words, being able to come to peace with our PAST and use our hopes for our FUTURE allows us to live a more kickass life in the NOW.

I am in. How about you?

For many of us, this approach is completely new. We are conditioned to beat ourselves up over our failures, to use the old line, "I will just do better the next time,". This prevents us from ever coming close to living a rich and meaningful life. We become too busy rehashing our failures and dooming ourselves in the process.

Are you ready for a change-up?

Great, let's go.

First, we need to redefine how we view goal-setting and apply these new strategies to increase our quality of life.

You deserve to have the life you desire.

The question is whether you are ready to let go of old ways of doing things, and commit to adopt new thought and feeling patterns, which will have positive effects in all areas of your life.

What I know for sure is this: being motivated is not enough to meet your goals; you must also have the capability to understand yourself more deeply and create opportunities for higher achievement in your life.

Nothing worth having occurs in a vacuum. We must examine all areas of our lives, especially the ones that aren't working. In order to create lasting change, we need to accept that we are a sum of all our experiences: past, present and future— the good, the bad, and the ugly.

How we create a vision and set goals is determined by our thoughts and emotions. Let's dig deeper into how we can use positive and affirming steps to achieve our breakthrough.

In order to experience positive change, we must embrace three stages in changing our behavior:

1. Awareness
2. Choice
3. Execution.

As a coach, nothing excites me more than seeing clients go from "I can't" to "I may" to "I will"!

Let's review these stages now.

First, *awareness.* For so many, it seems easier to stay in the dark! I get it. Facing the music and acknowledging that certain patterns, habits, and behaviors are detrimental to our wellbeing is tough to face. Many of my clients start working with me because they know they need the additional support to close the gap between where they are and where they want to be. These changes cannot happen in isolation.

Who will you draft for your support team? Who will keep it real for you? Who will tell you what behaviors are restricting your play to a small game and support you in creating an exciting vision for your future? Knowledge is power. The more you learn about yourself in this process, the greater your desire to live an unstoppable life will be. Mark my words.

First, you must look back and understand what got you in a jam so you are able to move more freely into the NOW.

Awareness is having the courage to look within and face your struggle so that you can move into the second stage of behavioral change: choice.

In the second phase, the *choice* stage, you are ready to face the music. To admit you are ready to make necessary changes enables you to take action steps towards your dreams and goals. Again, motivation is just not enough. There are too many obstacles and roadblocks to think you can will your way through big changes. The choice phase is a great time to create opportunities for yourself, so that you can experience personal wins and build on your inner confidence and self-efficacy.

Building our self-efficacy is making a commitment to renew and reignite our self-belief— that we are capable of making the changes necessary to be unstoppable and to make adjustments as needed to feel more vibrant and alive.

This stage is a great time to set goals and create an action plan to get you where you want to go. It's in the small shifts where our greatest transformations come alive. Belief in yourself is crucial here. You are worthy of meeting your goals. The clearer the vision, the more likely you will be able to reach it. Dream big, create the vision, and start living "as if". The power of affirmation cannot be denied.

For one of my clients, it was finally committing to give up the party lifestyle and drop 50 pounds of belly bloat. For another, it was to finally accept the fact that she was worthy of love and embracing the healthy lifestyle, so she could confidently meet the man of her dreams. And for another, accepting that the pain in his body wasn't about lack of flexibility or strength, but the stress from his work, enabled him to finally able to make the changes necessary to live a more balanced and peaceful existence.

The third stage, *execution* is exactly what the above clients committed to undertake. Was it easy? Definitely not. What is worth it for them? Judging by their current state of increased overall happiness and personal satisfaction in their lives, absolutely.

I believe the same for you.

Execution is all about putting your plan into action, step by step. Start small. The biggest successes start and end with micro-wins. Having people hold you accountable to your goals and vision is what helps the most successful people hit their goals out of the park.

Who do I suggest for an accountability partner? Someone who is also striving to be their highest and best self. This is about you getting your needs met, not dragging someone behind you on a sled, so make sure you both have clear goals and expectations for how you will serve and support each other.

Personally, I have always felt it was the best use of my time and resources to hire someone to hold me to the fire. I spread the responsibility between my business coach, fitness trainer, lawyer, accountant, and therapist to keep me on track to live my best life.

My success was not handed to me— not one bit. Behind my positive energy and drive to help as many people as possible reach their potential, is a person who has experienced tremendous loss, isolation, and personal and business failures. Yet nothing was bigger than my desire to be the biggest and baddest person on the block. Not because I want ego-boosting, to make a gazillion dollars, or all kinds of kudos (I am, in fact, way more of an ambivert than anyone who doesn't know me would believe).

Nope, I live like this every single day because I am looking for that person who needs a powerful mirror, so they can fall madly in love with themselves. I am clear on my calling. And that is why, no matter how calamity strikes, no matter what life throws my way, I am undaunted.

Are you ready to live life at that amazing place where pleasant life, engaged life, and deeply meaningful life converge?

My guess is that you are.

Be courageous enough to take the first step of faith, to move from "I can't" to the possibility of "I may". Let others join you, encourage you, and challenge you to the "I can!"

I believe in you. And its due time you believed in yourself as well.

Workbook #12:

1. What stories do you have on rewind and repeat in your mind? Is there a person you need to forgive? What do you have to forgive yourself for? Name it. Release the shame and reclaim your freedom.

____

____

____

____

____

2. What are you ready to accept and let go of?

3. Why is now the time to do that?

4. What does your life look like when you are living in alignment with your true self? What does it feel like?

THE TWO WORDS THAT WILL CHANGE YOUR LIFE

"Success at anything will always come down to this: focus and effort. And we control both." —Dwayne "The Rock" Johnson

Your overall approach to HOW you view your health and wellbeing matters, but what matters even more is WHAT you focus on. How do you define your own personal success and happiness? And more importantly, are you living it?

A lot of people define their success by making a to-do list and marking items off, no matter the degree of importance. And while many of us are extremely busy, the true question is: are you accomplishing what matters *the most* in order for you to have a happy and badass life?

Keeping busy and running around like a chicken with its head cut off is often a cover we use to avoid focusing on what is really most important in our lives: our health, wellbeing and the wealth of the relationships around us.

The truth is that at the end of the day, these are the things that matter most. Without our health and the richness of relationships, life can seem, well, pretty lackluster, to say the least!

You want to have an amazing life? If the answer is yes, it's time to get real on what you want. Secondly, you must start putting yourself in the equation by being honest with yourself and others about what you want in your life. Lastly, set your days, weeks, and months by ***radically prioritizing*** your time to attain the lifestyle you desire and deserve. These two words, ***radical prioritization***, once consistently applied, are guaranteed gamechangers.

A word of caution: when you decide to make yourself a priority, you're going to get all kinds of weird feedback from both the people around you and the powerful voices in your head, trust me.

"Who do you think you are?" "What do you think, you're special?" "People who focus on themselves are selfish." "You should put others' needs (your kids, your spouse, your parents) in front of your own." "I don't deserve it. I haven't worked hard enough, sacrificed enough, suffered enough…." Baloney!!!

My most successful clients— no matter if they're developing a business idea, leaving a toxic relationship, seeking the love of their life, building a healthy body, or letting go of self-sabotaging patterns and behaviors— all attain the greatest amount of success by finally being clear on:

1. WHY they want to make the change
2. ACCEPTING that they deserve it, then, finally,
3. RADICALLY PRIORITIZING the action steps to enthusiastically accomplish their goals.

Is attaining a life as a badass paved with daisies, bon-bons, and rainbows?

Heck, no!

Will there be days when you want to jump ship, go back to your days of running around like a maniac and end up binging ice cream and bad TV on the couch?

Sure.

However, once you decide that you have a clear purpose— a big and juicy "WHY" you would like to attain your vision and goals for yourself— combined with the right support and action steps, you will become unstoppable in your commitment to achieve anything your heart desires.

And how do I know this is true with such conviction?

In October of 2017, I experienced any parent's worst possible nightmare. My beautiful son, Will, took his own life in the White Mountains of New Hampshire. I was devastated. All those who knew and loved Will were and still remain devastated. But what I know for sure, with absolute certainty, is that Will would not want me, or any of those who loved him, to suffer. Yes, grief and loss is a heavy load to carry; however, long-term suffering, I believe, is optional.

So many of us have experienced the trials and tribulations in our lives. I understand this and have deep compassion for others. Because of my own personal experience with loss, I am now more than ever, committed to helping others attain the freedom and the joy of living an enthusiastic and fulfilling life.

Ready to apply the principles of ***radical prioritization***? I have compiled the following principles you can start applying today.

Workbook #13:

1. Make a list the night before of things you MUST accomplish the next day. If you know you won't get to your workout if you wait until later in the day, do it first thing upon rising. Sleep in your workout clothes if you have to (Trust me, I have done it!). Plan your meals and commit to feeding what fuels you. Tough conversations need to be had? Get it done

and end the hash-overs. The things on the list are your "must-do's", not your "somedays". Put the "somedays" on another page, so you don't get tempted to fall off track. At the end of the day, assess what you accomplished. Celebrate your wins, and please don't beat yourself up over the failures. Tomorrow is a new day. Leave yesterday's drama behind you. Self-flagellation is a complete time-waster. Please stop that.

2. Set realistic goals as to how long things are going to take. Ouch! This is a tough one for many of us, so lean on people to hold you accountable to stick to a plan. Hire a coach, trainer, use a timer, build in 15-minute windows of appointments, etc. It is a huge relief not to be under the gun all the time. Take stress and pressure off your plate. Be realistic on what you can get done. Do what you can, work efficiently, and take what you learned and confidently move forward. You got this!
3. Organize your space so you can function more efficiently. Successful people organize their lives around their purpose. Want to be a fit person? What area in your home or car needs to be organized so your fitness is automatic? How can you re-organize your cabinets and your shopping trips to make eating clean and healthy automatic? Does your bedroom look like an episode from *Storage Wars*? How are you welcoming in a new romantic relationship in that present condition? Money jammed in your wallet and receipts everywhere? Set a timer, and spend 15 minutes in these areas, and watch your life and attitude shift for the better.
4. Make yourself a ruthless priority. Silence the inner critic. Forgive yourself for past failures. The good news is when

we know better, we can choose to do better. Celebrate your wins, however small. Be your own biggest fan.

And remember, at the end of the end of the day, the three most important questions we can ask ourselves are the following:

1. Did I do my best?
2. Is there anyone I need to forgive? Do I need to forgive myself for anything?
3. Was I loving and kind to myself and others?

Tomorrow is a new day. Let's live in the hope and understanding that we all can make a difference. By putting yourself in the equation and living a life of *radical prioritizing*, you really can change your life and the lives of others for the better. You got this.

"When you realize how perfect everything is, you will tilt your head back and laugh at the sky." — Buddha

HOW TO WAKE UP AND CLAIM YOUR BEST LIFE

"Success consists of going from failure to failure without loss of enthusiasm." —Winston Churchill

Why is it that some people follow their dreams and achieve great success while others are barely squeezing by? Friends become excited by a great new idea, but by the next time you connect their enthusiasm has waned and they once again settle into the malaise of their ho-hum existence. Cripes, haven't we all been here? It feels as though we've driven as far as we were able to go and then, suddenly, pulled over and... parked.

As a coach, I hear the same defeated phrases over and over again from people: "I don't have time," "I already tried it, and it didn't work," "I just have bad luck." These are statements from people who have parked. How about you? Is there some area of your life where, perhaps, you have parked?

In the book *Grit*, by Angela Duckworth, the author highlights, from her own research, two important differentiations between those who succeed in life and those who don't. The two qualities are:

1. possessing a success mindset
2. adopting the power of resiliency.

The truth is, if you think you cannot, then you most likely won't. Similarly, if you expect to try to do something new, yet will only accept success as an end result, guess what? It's not going to work out too well for you either. In fact, you are better off planning to fail. In life you will, at some point, fail. You can ask any successful person if they have ever failed and you will hear some version of this age-old adage: "Failed? Ha! My success was paved in failure!" Based on my epic failures, I couldn't agree more.

My own life has been a series of failures, from small to colossal. Business ideas that fizzled out. Relationships that crumbled. Dreams dashed. Health tragedies. Personal crisis and loss more heart-wrenching than I ever could have imagined. Yet through all of this, I have also achieved some wonderful successes: amazing kids, the growth of a multi-million dollar business, appearing on national radio and TV, becoming a best-selling author, speaking in front of hundreds of people, coaching incredible clients, competing as an athlete, and being blessed with the most amazing friends a person could ever ask for.

I would not have been able to achieve this level of success without being willing, each time, to try again. Trying again despite the embarrassment and beating myself up over what I felt were horrible mistakes and miscalculations. It requires a mindset to still see the vision your heart desires while having the ability and conviction to get back up when you have been kicked down on your ass. And if I can do it, so can you.

Ask any of my clients, they will probably tell you this: "Kate believes in me, sometimes even more than I believe in myself." Knowing that this is what I do for others, my true purpose, is by far my biggest success in life. And I found my WHY through these many failures, often feeling alone and unsupported. And what I know for sure is this: we do not have to stumble alone. Heck, even the Lone Ranger had Tonto. The help is there for you. But first, you must wake up your desire to live your purpose, follow through, and be courageous enough to ask for the help and support you need.

Feeling unmotivated? Not even sure where to start? Here are five steps below to help you gain greater clarity to start living a life that reflects your true inner passion to succeed in life.

1. **Track your energy drains.** What are you tolerating in your life that needs to go? I have a worksheet I use with my clients that helps them start zapping tolerations—those little things in your life that sap your energy and time. Tolerating unorganized closets? Loose knobs? A messy car? A job that stinks? Attitude from someone in your family? Make now the time to take care of these tolerations, so you can enjoy a clearer mind and more peaceful and peace on a daily basis. (Check on the list of tolerations on page 16)
2. **Clear the clutter.** Get rid of old magazines, clothes, appliances, and sports equipment you no longer use. Schedule a weekly drop to your local donation center. Join one of the many online resale sites. Often, it's our plethora of "things" that make our visual space cluttered, preventing us from truly seeing what we want in our lives. Clarity is power. Make way for more joy and abundance by reducing the chaos all our extra stuff creates.
3. **Organize your ideas.** Start jotting down thoughts and dreams that come to you at random times in the day, no matter how silly the ideas seem. Reserve judgement on your ideas, no matter how far out in left field they appear. Notice what things excite you. Create time in your day for idle time, a space where you can hear yourself think and listen to your inner voice that is often drowned out in our everyday life. Dreams turn to reality when you add a powerful intention to them. Create a daily action plan to perform small steps to begin to attain all that your heart desires.

4. **Meditate/pray/commune/chill out.** Sitting quietly every day in silence is a challenging idea for many. The wandering monkey mind is real! It takes patience to set a practice. Give yourself permission to stumble through. This isn't some competition about how long you can sit still; it's simply knowing you took the time to be present enough and to observe your thoughts without judgement. What a powerful gift you can give yourself.

   Check out local meditation classes or download an app on your phone if you would like to have more instruction on how to develop your practice. There are so many tools out there to get you going. My recommendation is simply to start! It has changed my life. I look forward to hearing how it has changed yours.

5. **Rid your life of toxic relationships and habits.** There comes a time when you just can't pretend that the relationships around you are healthy and bringing out your best self. Same thing with habits that are depleting your energy, eating up all your resources, and making you foggy and self-delusional. You deserve to have a healthy relationship and a body free from toxins that put your dreams to sleep. There are coaches and therapists out there waiting to help you launch your life to a new level. People who will believe in you and support you through your transformation. Is now your time to seek the assistance you deserve?

Success happens one small step at a time. And yes, you will be knocked down. And yes, people will turn away from you. And yes, you will sometimes feel unsure and alone. The good news is: once you wake up, going back to sleep— forgetting who you are and who you came here to be— is no longer an option. Things that you once tolerated will no longer stand in your way. Your mind will be clearer, your life richer.

At the end of the day, nothing beats putting your head on the pillow, knowing you did all you could to live your best life, even if it didn't exactly turn out as planned...

Workbook #14:

1. Where in your life are you feeling drained of energy and unmotivated?

____

____

____

____

____

____

2. Where do you feel that energy drain in your body?

____

____

____

3. In the past, how have you been able to lift yourself up when feeling down?

4. Is there an area in your house that needs some cleaning out? Set a by-when date on when you will get this done. Spending five to ten minutes a day to chunk out this project is a great tool that I use to approach feelings of overwhelm. It really works!

5. Do you have a daily meditation/prayer practice? If so, what does it look like? If not, what would you like to start to do daily to sit quietly with yourself that feels challenging yet inspiring? Find an area in your home where you can do that and begin today.

____

____

____

____

____

____

6. What relationships in your life are draining you? Are there conversations you need to have that you have been putting off? How can you approach these conversations with a resilient and positive mindset, and become less attached to the others' reactions? Picture how you want these conversations to go, and keep your intentions clear, no matter their response. Stay with the intention of love.

____

____

____

____

____

WHEN QUITTING IS NOT AN OPTION

> *"Stay on track, don't look back. You have come too far not to finish what you started. You can improve, you can change, you can progress, you can make a difference. You can do it, if you stay on track." — Germany Kent*

You started the day, week, month, year with all kinds of resolve and fire to meet and beat a kickass goal and now after an hour, a day, a week, a month, you feel your commitment waiver and the dreaded march of retreat into the maligned "someday, but not today" thinking. Comfort begins to take precedence over your goals to be your best self. Ugh! One of my most loathed word in the English language: "someday"!

As your coach, I plead with you: Please don't quit. You decided on this goal for a specific reason— to feel stronger, wealthier, healthier, wiser. So, what has changed? Why do so many of us pull over on the side of the road and park? The problem that so few people talk about is that motivation will only get you so far. That is why it is crucial to create a plan that takes over when your motivation wanes, so you can get yourself all the way to the finish line.

Let's go over the components of what it takes to make your dreams not only possible, but a reality, by learning how to hijack your thinking at the exact point when your motivation leaves the building.

The methodology I have developed takes a holistic approach to getting there. While good nutrition, exercise, vision creation, and goal-setting are important and key elements to the plan, your inner "mojo" (that "something" that makes you tick and sets you on fire) is the foundation of rocking your goals and living the breakthrough life you deserve.

What happens on the inside— your emotions, self-talk, patterns, and behaviors— have a direct impact on how you look and feel on the outside. That is why I emphasize so strongly the importance of cultivating your "mojo", the inner magic that moves us beyond our limited thinking.

Transformation is an inside job. Sure, your *will* and *desire* to succeed are important aspects of success. *But truly the most important element of any transformation is fully accepting that you are worthy to live your life all-out and to stay committed, even when the desire to do the work has flown the coop!*

In the following section, I highlight six ways you can overcome the brain fog that sets in when you lose your motivation. Ways to disrupt your stinkin' thinkin'. These strategies work— start applying them today, and keep reaching for the stars!

SIX STEPS TO KICK OVERWHELM TO THE CURB

"You can't calm the storm, so stop trying. What you can do is calm yourself. The storm will pass." — Timber Hawkeye

We have all been there. You can't think straight, you feel weepy, irritated, foggy, and weary. Everything seems to irritate you and you can't put your finger on exactly what it is. Yup, you are in overwhelm, the state of being when your brain feels like it has blown a transformer and you are left standing in the dark, no idea what to do next.

When in overwhelm, our brain, as magical and amazing as it is, doesn't see our long list of to-do's, our stressed out conversations with others, our rushing to get to an appointment— what our brain senses is imminent threat and then... pfissh— out goes the lights, all circuitry is down!

When in that state of complete overwhelm, our brain resorts to survival mode— fight, flight, or freeze. These three reactions are exactly where our most unproductive habits and behaviors are born and, unfortunately, thrive.

Flight is the most sneaky, as it can manifest in all kinds of habits that "look" productive; however, at a closer look, these habits are often preventing us from getting what really is most important, done. Flight habits can override the positive habits that help us attain greater satisfaction in our lives on a daily, even moment-to-moment basis.

When overwhelmed, we use all kinds of interesting tactics to look and feel productive in order to avoid our fear of failure, disappointing others, or feeling incapable— emotional states that fuel our desire to avoid the truth of what is.

Why do I teach on this point so often in my business as a coach? Why can I spot overwhelm in others a million miles away? Because in life, we are often drawn to teach on the lessons in those areas we personally need to grow the most. I know overwhelm so well I could have a PhD in it!

Please remember that you are not alone. Others have felt just like you: isolated and trapped in a similar cycle of defeat. I tell you that not to make light of your suffering, but to reach out a hand of hope. I do believe that there is a way out for you, as there was for me.

Below are five action steps to help you boot overwhelm to the curb, and live the rich and juicy life you deserve *and* long for.

1. **Breathe.** Yep, just breathe. Not just breathe in, but breathe out, too. So many of us spend our days holding our breath, without even realizing it. Check in right now. Are you breathing fully in and out? The pace of our lives has become so hectic that we have even forgotten to breathe! How crazy is that??

Try this: As you breathe in, think of a calming word, like peace, flow, allow, trust. As you breathe out, use words or phrases like release, let go, all is well, yes, or any other that allows you to stop the mental madness and be present in the "now".

Even just one good belly breath can actually change your whole mental zip code. Try it.

Workbook #15:

1. What word(s) makes you feel a greater sense of calm?

____

____

____

____

____

Remember it only takes one deep breath in and out to bring the monkey mind to rest and bring peace/God/serenity in. Even if this is hard for you to fathom right now, could you trust me enough right now to just try it?

2. **Repeat after me:** "This, too, shall pass." It's true. In our moments of complete chaos, it's important to remember that you had peace before this moment, and peace will surely return again. Oftentimes, things need to unravel in order to reveal who we are truly meant to be. Trust in the process. You are going to be okay. Really.

Can you remember a time in your life where you felt peaceful? Can you describe that moment in time? What were you doing? Who were you with?

____

____

Where does peace and calm show up in your body? Where do you feel it?

3. **Allow.** Allow the feeling of overwhelm to come to the surface. Then, as you deep belly breathe, name the other emotions that hide underneath and around the feeling of overwhelm (these could be fear, sorrow, grief, terror, even relief and happiness). By naming these other emotions and seeing them for what they are, we can set ourselves free from their grip. Go ahead: name them and set yourself free. It's due time.

Can you name the emotion as it arises?

Can you allow yourself to sit in that emotion and allow it to rise, welcome it, and, then, feel it dissipate?

4. **Write it down.** Make a list— however haphazard— of everything. I mean EVERYTHING you have in your head, whether it is a to-do, a to-don't, and everything in between.

Now look at the list and separate it into themes, areas of your life, a timeline, or whatever way resonates with you. Trust your gut here. Everyone's process is different. Honor yours. Cross off the items that are not yours to do. Delegation is an art form. Practice will make perfect.

Whether you are a CEO in a corporation, own your own business, or are an at-home parent, learning to break down our to-do's is a great way to free yourself from overwhelm and create a plan to get yourself cracking. Free your mind by putting pen to paper.

Do you have a journal, a favorite pen you like to use? Is there a place in your home you feel most safe and, perhaps, free? Choose a place to sit and do your brain dump from all the noise in your head. Then, after sitting and sorting this list, review and create action steps to start chipping away, one small task at a time. I call this my "divide and conquer" list. This process has been instrumental for my clients. Please try it out, and let me know how it works for you.

5. **Stop multitasking**. Multitasking is an illusion. It is procrastination at its highest form. Stop the madness, pronto. Being present with what you are doing in each moment is the biggest gift you can give yourself and others. Do you feel drawn to check your phone 100 times a day or Google search for more time than you are comfortable admitting? Are you thinking of other things when communicating with others? Just as we do in mindfulness meditation, simply notice where your monkey mind is taking you. Just notice. Don't beat yourself up, shame yourself, or feel guilty. Your greatest transformation will happen in loving kindness, not self-abuse. So, be loving to yourself. Haven't you beat yourself up long enough? Why not make NOW the time to let go of behaviors that break down your spirit, instead of lifting you up? I would say it's due time.

Observe how it feels to do a couple tasks one at a time. What emotions come up for you? Even completing a couple tasks being wholly present will shift your mindset into a more peaceful space.

____

____

____

____

____

When performing several things at a time, are your thoughts more past or future-based? How can you shift your conscious awareness to be more present-based?

____

____

____

____

____

6. **Hire a coach/find an accountability partner**. Find a person in your life who will help you stay out of overwhelm and keep you in action. Set parameters on how you want to support each other. Be honest and kind in your interactions by holding each other at your highest and best. Nothing beats having someone to celebrate with!

Having a coach over the last several years has allowed me to attain a level of success that I could only have dreamed of before. I learned how to define and communicate my needs, how to be laser clear on my goals. By becoming clear on how I wanted to live my life daily, I was able to say "ta-ta!" to many behaviors that contributed to my perpetual state of overwhelm. Clarity is definitely power.

Are you ready for the same? My clients are a living, breathing testament of what hiring a coach can do to get you performing at your highest level. The cloud of overwhelm is just a veil that can be lifted whenever you are ready to make the commitment to be your highest and best self.

Overwhelm basks in confusion and adores inaction. Don't fall for its sneaky guise! By taking these six action steps today, you will be that much closer to living a life filled with the peace and happiness you deserve. Your breakthrough life awaits!

SET YOURSELF FREE FROM SELF SABOTAGE

"If you are insecure, guess what? The rest of the world is, too. Do not overestimate the competition and underestimate yourself. You are better than you think." — T. Harv Eker

You get all fired up about beginning a new diet and exercise program, looking for a new career, writing a book, whatever your next BIG thing is and after some time, *woosh...* your enthusiasm flies out the window.

And then it happens: that same old nasty inner critic rears its ugly head. You start hearing the same tape again and again, repeating in a familiar voice, *What is the matter with you? Stop being such a loser. You will never amount to anything.* You feel yourself fill with doubt and dread, and become frozen in disappointment and fear.

Sound familiar?

The trigger could be exhaustion, a fight with your significant other, bad traffic, a big change at work, misbehaving kids, or nothing at all. But the results are the same. You start skipping workouts, binging on desserts, stop showing up to places where you would be held accountable, and cutting yourself down with a litany of cruel and negative self-talk.

And here lies the number one deal dasher: self-sabotage. I see it with so many of my clients. It is, by far, the most frequent subject I coach around: how we self-sabotage and how you can manage this process. Managing this is imperative for staying on track to pursue your goals and preventing yourself from falling into the trap of your monkey mind of self-destruction.

Self-sabotage can happen to anyone, even the most successful people you know. The key is to prepare a strategic plan to distract and diminish self-defeating thinking, habits, and behaviors so you can continue on as the warrior you came here to be.

It's important to first touch on why we are so swayed by self-sabotage, so we can disrupt the patterns that derail us. Research shows self-sabotaging behaviors are largely unconscious. By and large, we act, create, manifest, and attract according to our self-concept, or who we believe ourselves to be. Many times, self-sabotaging actions stem from fear. Fear of failure, rejection, change, other people's opinions, and even fear of success!

As a coach, I have some time-proven strategies to share that you can apply when feeling like you are stuck in a pattern of self-destruction. They work with my clients, and I can guarantee that these strategies will also work for you.

So, the next time you feel the urge to self-destruct and blow up your best-laid plans: stop, take a chill pill, and apply this five-step process.

1. **Reflect on your emotional state.** Are you feeling sad, angry, stressed, jealous, lonely, unworthy, fearful, celebratory or happy? That's right! Even in our happier moments, we can abandon our goals. It's important to acknowledge these feelings, so they can be validated and dealt with, instead of buried and ignored. Once we confront our real feelings, we can consciously choose to fulfill our needs in ways that support our goals. Journal, start a mood tracker, anything that helps you lovingly self-reflect.

2. **Ask yourself "why".** Now that you've uncovered the underlying emotions you're experiencing, the next step is to figure out why they are bubbling to the surface. What are your self-perceptions that cause this self-defeating pattern of behavior to occur? Is food your only consistent form of pleasure, leading you to binge? Are you afraid of judgement if you speak your truth to someone you care about? Are you feeling exposed or judged by diving into a new project or job opportunity? What is the intention behind the self-defeating behavior? The binging may be happening to help you cope with stress, to experience feelings of comfort, companionship, or relief. Often, just acknowledging these emotions and their roots is enough to set yourself free.
3. **Choose another course of action**. Self-sabotaging can be a difficult habit to break. We tend to revert back to familiar behaviors, no matter how detrimental they may be, if we do not have an alternative plan in place. Once we define what it is we crave, we can hone in on some tactics to divert our attention elsewhere.

   For example, a change of scenery or talking to a friend can alter our perspective on a situation that has us stressed out. Sometimes, all it takes is a 10-minute walk around your neighborhood to re-calibrate. Replace late night snacking in front of the TV with reading in bed. If you're feeling unworthy or unloved, pamper yourself with a hot shower, deep conditioning treatment, and a luxurious home manicure/pedicure with a bright, new polish. You deserve that level of self-care!

4. **Find a New Tribe.** When motivation wanes, one of the greatest things we can do is ask for help. To ensure long-term success, it's important to have someone to check in

with, such as a health and lifestyle coach and/or a licensed mental health clinician. Sharing our goals and struggles with others tends to encourage us to stay on course, helps to reframe our negative thoughts, and allows us to recognize potentially unrealistic expectations. Promising to meet a friend for a workout, joining a Meetup group, or becoming part of a professional networking group are fantastic ways of ensuring we show up for ourselves. It's much more difficult to blow off our goals when we know it also means letting down friends and colleagues.

5. **Think beyond you.** Sometimes, we get stuck on ourselves and think the world notices all of our flaws with the magnitude that we do. We forget that we are human and we are allowed to make mistakes. Many of us compare ourselves to others, fixate on the differences and flag them as perceived shortcomings. Our inner critic is constantly yammering away, pointing these things out to us, but he/she has forgotten one important detail— we are all meant to be different. We are each on our own journey in this lifetime. When you get down on yourself, think about who else may be watching and learning from you— your kids, your clients, your friends?

Instead of focusing on your own negative self-talk, imagine what it would be like to be an inspiration to your community. When you find that dream job, complete that boot camp, or find a healthy relationship that lights you up, it will trigger feelings of belief and enthusiasm in others that could, quite possibly, drive them to take positive action. How cool is that?

Helpful tip: Think about someone who inspires you and try to emulate their character traits. It really helps if you make a list and start adopting those values you admire.

Remember that nobody is perfect and your path to achieve greatness needs to be flexible and fluid. Don't fall into the trap of black-and-white, all-or-nothing thinking. Putting an end to self-sabotage starts with believing in yourself and knowing you are capable of a life beyond your wildest dreams.

Workbook #16:

1. Tune into what your body is telling you when you start feeling a sense of dread. Where are you feeling and emotions?

____

____

____

____

____

2. What voice are you hearing? Is it your own voice or someone else's? Make note. Often, our most damaging tapes we are hearing are not even our own.

____

____

____

____

____

3. What habits can you adopt to break self-sabotaging behaviors? (Ideas: a quick walk around the block, a call to a friend, mediating, dancing, watching or reading something light-hearted or funny).

"No one can make you feel inferior without your consent." —
Eleanor Roosevelt

That's something to ponder…

Letting Go of Fear to Live a Positive Lifestyle

"New beginnings are often disguised as painful endings." — Lao Tzu

Fear is essential: it protects us when needed. However, having it be a "go-to" emotion will only short-circuit your life. Fear can be extremely motivating and energizing, helping you push through barriers, persist, and work hard to achieve a goal; yet, so many are encased in it, like they are locked in a tomb with no way out.

The key to freedom from a constant state of fear will not be found on social media, maybe not even from a family member or a friend. The key to your freedom is in acceptance of where you are and trusting that things will work out for you if you let the need to control go. Control is the lock *and* the key. It's time to let that go.

Let fear speak to you, but don't speak with fear. Notice it, say hello to it, even welcome it with a smile. Fear is the part of you that is afraid to be vulnerable, of being abandoned, controlled, or manipulated. The fear is really just a call to love.

Often fear is just a mask of anxiety, covering what was or could be. We spend so much time worrying about what could or couldn't happen, why we said this or that— we lose so much time *living*.

Isn't it time for you to be free from obsessing about the past and/or worrying about the future? Let's commit to welcoming aliveness, joy, and compassion into our lives. Here are some ways to reframe fear and live with more acceptance and peace of mind:

1. **Do not fight fear.** Embrace this emotion with tenderness, as though embracing a baby. Your humanness is influenced by an array of emotional experiences. The problem is that we get fixated on one state of being, limiting our ability to function in a healthy way. Be an observer of your emotions. Become a master of your emotional experiences. Lighten up on the self-judgement and adopt a lighter treatment of yourself— one that includes laughter and self-forgiveness.

2. **Plant seeds.** Water your own beautiful seeds of goodness and the seeds of others. We have the power to choose which seeds to water. Recognize that we all have seeds of fear, but we have the power to transform them. Be clear on how you want to experience life, and start living your days with that intention. Then, seek and celebrate these attributes in others.

3. **Look at fear with the energy of mindfulness.** Be able to recognize the roots of suffering in the people you love. Untying internal knots requires discernment of your fear from the fear of others. Are you taking on their experiences more than necessary to your detriment? Don't run away from it; bring it up and take a good look at it. We cover it, distract ourselves, and ignore it.

By embracing it with mindfulness, you can then transform it. Mindfulness is observing and paying attention to something while letting go of judgments and assumptions. Breathing in and out consciously helps you become your best, calmest, freshest, most solid, clear self. Coming home to your body, your body informs you. Mindfulness helps us taste the joy of each moment very deeply. Mindfulness is the energy that helps us to be here 100 percent. True presence. Mindfulness is the practice of living in a place of love and compassion made out of one substance: *understanding.*

4. **Reframe your language.** Stop using these toxic phrases:

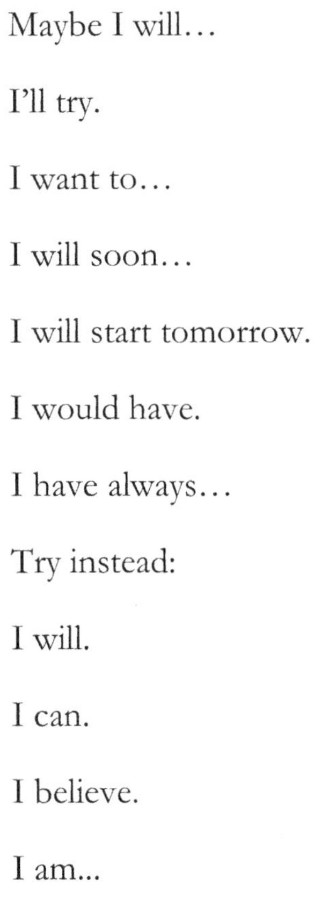

Maybe I will…

I'll try.

I want to…

I will soon…

I will start tomorrow.

I would have.

I have always…

Try instead:

I will.

I can.

I believe.

I am...

Affirming statements have the ability to transform your state of being. Listen to how you speak, and make these small words shifts to radically change your life.

5. **Stop thinking that just venting or getting it off your chest makes things better.** It actually often makes it worse, because after you calm down from your vent, the self-doubt, embarrassment, and regret sets in. You spend hours reviewing and

deciding the next step is passing on the venom to others by trying to build a consensus with your family and friends. Start owning your stuff.

What seeds are you cultivating by the way you live your life and how you treat others? Joy, peace, and happiness are possible. Shaming, blaming, and complaining are just our ways to deflect from our truth: that we want to love and be loved. Could it be that simple? I believe that it is.

"Everything outside of love can be turned back into love. Love that is pure and true." --Will Boynton (my son, who passed on his own accord 10/14/17)

UNDERSTANDING COGNITIVE DISSONANCE TO BOOST YOUR BADASSERY

"Times of great calamity and confusion have been productive for the greatest minds. The purest ore is produced from the hottest furnace. The brightest thunderbolt is elicited from the darkest storm." — Charles Caleb Colton

Every day, we are presented with decisions that may or may not align with our core beliefs. The process we use to make decisions can be pretty effortless when the decisions are not "do-or-die"; however, when we are forced to make bigger decisions, ones that may affect our health, finances, or relationships, many of us freeze in indecision. We feel our inner emotional state laced with profound fear and dread.

And what do we fear most? Feelings of doubt and regret: two natural human emotions that actually aid our decision-making process— only if we are open to a deeper exploration into our personal awareness.

What often happens is that we are going along in our life with everything moving along smoothly, then suddenly, our emotional state gets hijacked: all circuitry goes haywire when we experience *cognitive dissonance.*

Cognitive dissonance is the experience of discomfort that results from opposing attitudes and/or behaviors. According to

Leon Festinger (1957), cognitive dissonance theory suggests that we have an inner desire to hold all our attitudes and behaviors in harmony and avoid disharmony. For example, someone who smokes (behavior) knows that smoking causes cancer (cognition), therefore, they are in a state of cognitive dissonance. In order to relieve this state and return to a state of harmony, something must change.

We can do the following to retain emotional harmony:

1. Change. (i.e. quit smoking, stop binge-eating, stop picking the wrong person to date, quit gambling)

2. Acquire new information that outweighs the dissonant beliefs. (Bargaining away our behaviors and habits by finding statistical justification)

3. Reduce the importance of cognition. ("Hey, we only live once." "I can start my diet tomorrow." etc.)

How to move through these life challenges, however big or small, is key to living like a badass. And how you choose to resolve the dissonance and its accompanying discomfort is a reflection of your emotional wellbeing. Viewing these challenges as an opportunity for growth allows you to embrace your full range of emotions. This informs your life path going forward.

Below are four steps you can apply to make decisions in your life with greater confidence. As a result, you may find yourself adopting a deeper sense of personal power:

1. **Expect some doubt and regret as a possible outcome to any decision you make.** These are natural human emotions. Let them inform you, not nail you to your current predicament. You are not a tree. You can pick up and change at any time. It is our own right to change our mind. Judge yourself less. You are human, and you are growing—celebrate all aspects of your process of discernment with humor and grace. This process of acceptance is one of the greatest gifts of being human.

2. **When weighing out a decision, imagine the downside of each possibility.** What this does is minimize the negative experience *if* (and perhaps *when*) things don't work out as planned. Information is power, both mentally and emotionally. If you are willing to face ALL that is possible in your life, you are less likely to freeze in indecision and fear when meeting obstacles on your new path. Moving confidently towards your new way of being is easier the more informed and aware you are. Good for you for committing to the best version of you.

3. **Remain flexible.** Expand your horizons to account for all possibilities when moving forward with a life change. For example, you set a goal to lose ten pounds before your high school reunion. It is important to take into consideration not only the variables, such as your changes in diet and exercise, but also the emotional changes you will experience as you move through your transformation.

As a coach, where most people fall down is when they are pulled to old habits (late night binging, blowing off the gym, dating another jerk, buying another pair of shoes, not following up on sales leads), and they revert to bargaining and justifying their backward slide. This is the time where a coach or an accountability partner is key. Flexibility is understanding that there will be resistance, that you *will* be pulled back to old behaviors; however, you understand and accept that course-correcting is always an option at any given moment. Define yourself not by your failures, but by your ability to fall and get back up again, without a loss of enthusiasm. You got this.

4. **Be prepared for resistance.** People will judge you, undermine you, and expect you to fail when you decide to make a bold change in your life. And the most shocking part of this? The people who supposedly love you the most are often the least likely to be the ones cheering you on. People will resist your change, no matter what your resolve. Your best defense? Be prepared for the resistance by planning your statement of intent. Declare your decision with confidence and resolve. If you are clear on why you are making these changes and knowing that it serves your highest, best self, you will be less swayed by someone's temper tantrum or even your own self-sabotage. It's your time to live your best life. You can attain this by staying true to your best version of YOU.

By embracing the pros and cons of your decision, your ability to stay committed will be increased, despite both internal and external resistance. Cognitive dissonance is a natural part of personal transformation. Expect and embrace it by preparing your approach, and remember to stay open to all the wonder and humor that life offers us.

Onward, Badass!

P.O.P. YOUR WAY TO SUCCESS!

"One important key to success is self-confidence. An important key to self-confidence is preparation." –Arthur Ashe

Have you heard of the old expression "luck is where preparation meets opportunity"? I don't know about you, but I view luck like I do hope— some far-off, distant thing, outside of my control. As a coach, I help people every day take their goals and aspirations to the next level, and to be honest, hope and luck have nothing on the determination in my clients' faces when they have set their intention and are ready to move fully into their goals and dreams.

Success is built on preparation and opportunity for sure, but there is one element missing from this formula and without it, our odds of success are greatly reduced. And what is that secret sauce? I call it *positive expectancy*— the belief and confidence that things are going to work out in our favor (and if they don't, we will be able to roll with the results).

Now, that is not to say that things don't go wrong— I am living proof that no matter how positive a mindset is, situations still fall apart and failure happens… a lot. Failure is a way of life for the most successful.

At a recent speaking event, a participant shared a story about how she has used positive expectancy in her favor. Her coach helped her create a system where she approaches her golf swing with confidence, and whether she nails the swing or not, she knows she is doing her best. This allows her to accept a poor swing with less angst. The game of golf is a great metaphor in how we can approach challenges in any area of our lives, be it health and wellness, relationships, or even business goals.

As long as we approach life's events with a clear vision of our desired outcome, the end result becomes way less dramatic; especially if you have learned how to adapt your strategy and keep on swinging through the highs and lows.

So, are you ready for a change-up? Are you ready to get fit, lose weight, or improve your relationships? How about finding more fulfilling work? Making more moolah? Are you itching for more and, yet, have been hesitant to say it out loud, because you fear judgement or that you're not worthy? As a lifestyle and business coach, I have seen this time and time again: feelings of unworthiness or lack of confidence are often at the root of people's unhappiness and dissatisfaction.

This is the reason why I have created a system of success based on the acronym P.O.P., which outlines the winning strategies you can apply to any area of your life, just like my most successful clients.

I want to see you win. Let's take steps together to achieve the life you deserve. Are you ready?

Here goes:

1. **Preparation**: What is it that you want? Really. Like "embarrassed to say it out loud" want? What I suggest to my clients is to write it down. Journal, and then share this goal with a mentor, a coach, or a friend you can trust. A big part of beginning a success journey is putting it out there in the Universe and, then, taking small, daily action to get there. And, then, being on watch for gifts on your path to start showing up. Be flexible on your path, but stay focused

on what you desire as an outcome. For example, you wanted to lose five pounds last month, and you ended up losing three. Yet, you feel amazing and scored your first push-up. That is a win. Or you applied for a new job, and you were rejected, yet "out of the blue" you were offered a new position at your company that challenges and delights you. Another win. At the front end, you may not know exactly what the gift will look like, but trust that setting your intention and putting it out there really does have some magic in it.

2. **Opportunity**: is a set of circumstances that makes it possible to do something. In other words, opportunity is something that you create, and not something to wait for. Success does not grow in a vacuum; you must actively live into it. What must you put into place now, so you can achieve all that you desire?

Creating the right opportunity means having the necessary items to gather and be ready to roll. For example: You want to get fit, so you can have a more enjoyable summer: decide on an exercise plan that works best for you; hire a coach to keep you on task and/or a trainer to design your fitness plan; remove all the junk food in your house, so that you are not tempted to binge; set your workout clothes out the night before, so you are ready to go first thing. A new job? Redo the résumé that needs updating, reach out to people you haven't talked to in a while in your chosen field, join a networking group. Be and do things that will put you in the right place, at the right time. So when opportunity does knock, will you be ready?

Positive Expectancy- the belief that things are going to work out in your favor, and if they do not work out according to plan, you will be nimble in your ability to adapt and bounce back from adversity. The truth is, it's not enough to be motivated by external factors (i.e. how you look, how other people perceive you). We must focus on internal beliefs that lay the groundwork so we can achieve what we truly want and desire. And by focusing on your outcome in a positive light, from the inside out, you are far less likely to be swayed by peer pressure, negative self-talk, and repeating old patterns of behavior that no longer serve you.

Also, approaching situations in a positive light adds joy to our lives. Fun is motivating! Plus, we can't fake fun; have you ever tried? It just doesn't work.

Approaching life with positive expectancy doesn't mean we think life is just all about unicorns and rainbows; certainly Polly Anna, I am not. However, I do believe my ability to shift my energy internally to a more positive state has allowed me to succeed at a much higher level (and have way more fun doing it). If I can do it, so can you.

What does success look like to you? Are you ready to live it? As always, I am here cheering you on from the sidelines. By applying these steps outlined above, I believe you can shift your life from ho-hum to outrageous. Start today to open your channels to a better life. Watch: the fog will lift; I guarantee you will be pleased by what you see and experience. It probably won't look like what you expect, but trust— yes, trust— that you deserve and are ready for way more than what you have been settling for.

BADASSERY AND BODY IMAGE- HOW TO REBOOT YOUR STINKIN' THINKIN'

"There is a direct correlation between positive energy and positive results in the physical form."
— Joe Rogan

So many of us are seeking to be at our "ideal weight". We feel that if we reach that weight, we can finally be happy. So, we try every fad diet and exercise regimen, thinking we will surely get it right this time.

And what happens with those "lucky few" who actually reach their weight loss goals? That number on the scale becomes a near obsession. Doing everything possible to stay there and keep that weight off. These people may isolate themselves, create hyper-rigid nutritional guidelines, and attempt to stay within this vigilant lifestyle plan. They keep this up until they either experience a health crisis, an injury that takes them out of their game or they crack and completely let go, reverting back to their old patterns of eating and end up gaining the weight back (and then some).

I promise you, there is another way. And it begins with a different mindset and a new approach. This is an acceptance to being your best self and it begins with self-love, not self-abuse. This castigating self-treatment just doesn't work, or we would be a world no longer overflowing with diet how-to's and "lose weight now" slogans. Add social media to the fray, and we are, as a culture, nearly sunk.

Are you one of those people? Maybe you don't feel good about yourself and feel that everything you've tried hasn't worked? Are you ready to let this pattern go and embrace a life where you are finally able to unleash your inner badass?

Why is it that in so many other areas of our lives we can accept *normal, average* or *good,* but when it comes to our body, we hold ourselves to a totally different standard? Even using the word "ideal" when we are talking about our body, a word defined as "absolute perfection", sets us up for a forever-seeking and never satisfied cycle of negative self-worth and disappointment.

The weight-loss industry, a multi-billion-dollar engine, feeds our disgruntled self-image, that part of us that feels forever dissatisfied once again at our lack of willpower and resolve.

But what if we have it all wrong? What if we actually turn this whole "get skinny and, then, be happy" paradigm on its head and start from being happy with who we are from the start, and set our goals for health and wellness from there? It sounds almost revolutionary, doesn't it?

So much of my work as a coach is helping my clients get to their "happy place". We do this by talking about then reframing beliefs about who they are and how they perceive themselves. I've realized the messages we send to ourselves are shocking! Certainly, we wouldn't talk to our friends and family that way!

The truth of the matter is this: Happiness can only exist when we fully commit to being kind to ourselves in how we show up today, not when we were 20, not in six months, but right now.

Are you ready to jump off this crazy diet cycle and finally have peace and happiness? I know I was.

After twelve years as a competitive athlete, with strict nutrition and exercise parameters, I have had to, over the last year, set a new "ideal" for myself. The process has definitely not been an easy one. But I had to practice what I preach.

What I know now— with even greater clarity— is that my happiness is not based on being competition-ready; my happiness is based on where I am right now, this moment. From this place, I decide how I am going to nourish myself: body, mind, and spirit.

Through my own research and through my work with clients, I've learned it's important to practice some form of daily meditation or prayer practice. My practice has helped me and millions of others "reboot" our thinking and re-set self-perception in ways that have changed lives. Are you ready to give it a try?

My biggest commitment in life is to help others come to believe that it is possible that we can create a paradigm shift in being happy with who we are in this moment, to live the healthy life we deserve, in a body that is strong, fueled with good nutrition, positive self-image, and peace. That, to me, is the consummate definition of what being a badass is all about.

It's your time. Go out and live your best badass self.

Workbook #17:

1. When in your life have you been healthiest in your own body self-image?

____

____

____

2. What does happiness mean to you?

3. Studies show that your happiness increases when you reach out and help others. Who in your life is struggling that could use a boost, a call, a text, a coffee date, or an errand run? Make a list, and attend to one or two a day. Watch your happiness in your own life increase.

4. If I am not my self-sabotaging thoughts, what am I?

____

____

____

____

____

5. Why is now the best time to let go of self-destructive thoughts and behaviors?

____

____

____

____

____

Hands-on Feels Exercise

This exercise described below is not easy for some, but the potential feel-good gains are huge. Sit in a relaxed position, and put your hands on your heart or your belly, breathe in deeply, and repeat quietly to yourself, "I am *peaceful*" (or whatever feel-good word works for you). Now, let that vibration move through your body, radiating out from where you sit. Continue to breathe in and out, until you can picture the energy field filling your whole world around you. Now, go move into your day. You got this.

"Always trust your instincts, they are messages from your soul, they are that inner part of you that strives to make you whole." — Anonymous

Reclaim Your Body, Reclaim Your Life – How to Say Adios to Low Self-Esteem

"You yourself, as much as anybody in the entire universe, deserve your love and affection." —Sharon Salzburg

When we are ready to claim our badassery, it is important not only to focus our attention on nutrition and exercise, but also on the role that healthy self-esteem and a positive body image plays on our ability to embrace a healthy lifestyle.

So much conversation in our society, supported and promoted by the media, focuses on looking a certain way and measuring our bodies on an "ideal" body type.

Let's be real.

How many of us truly fit into this "ideal" that is portrayed and extolled in the media? And more importantly, how many of us accept the body that we have in all its uniqueness?

Our bodies are all different, yet we hold ourselves to some "ideal" that is not only unrealistic for the majority of us, but also potentially dangerous to our health.

Ideal (n) - A standard of perfection; something in its perfection

Why is that we can be satisfied with our "personal best" in many other areas of our lives, but when it comes to our weight and fitness level, we become paralyzed, even obsessed with some illusory sense of our "ideal" body? Often, as a result of this incongruence, our own sense of self-worth and self-acceptance plummets.

As a coach, I am often asked about the latest fad diet and best exercise plan. But the conversation most often turns to the more painful truth: that of self-doubt, frustration, and even self-loathing. This is crushing to hear.

So many of us think that if we just lose 20 pounds, make more money, find that relationship, land a new job, we will finally be happy,

I am here to tell you that self-acceptance and self-love is a choice you can make in this moment, with the body you have and within the circumstances you are currently living.

We can do this by having a healthier body image and embracing positive self-esteem, so we can enjoy— once and for all— the peace and joy we want and deserve in this moment.

Here are some steps you can take to embrace this self-love lifestyle. Is it easy? Not at all. In fact, for many, this is one of the most difficult things you will ever do. But you deserve this, you really do. And the hardest part is to bust through resistance and begin. But I am right here beside you, cheering you on.

Here goes:

1. **See yourself as a whole person.** We are all a conglomerate of mixes and matches of our DNA, family, and life experiences. When you really stop to think about it, you have been through a lot, haven't you? When you look at it from that perspective, doesn't it seem kind of silly to judge yourself so harshly, especially when you look at yourself in

the mirror? Instead of focusing on the body parts that offend you, how about loving on the parts of you that are beautiful? How about reminding yourself of the qualities that make you up as a person that people compliment you on? You are a whole being—not just your thighs, your attitude, or your net worth. Embrace your whole self. Take a bird's eye view. You are beautiful.

2. **Celebrate what is unique about you.** Again, focus on what's unique about you, and don't be afraid to show those parts to the world. How strange it was to discover that the parts of me I was trying to hide were actually my innate and wonderful gifts. Who knew that what I viewed as a big mouth and outgoing personality is exactly why I have achieved great success in my life, because people depend on me to tell the truth, that they can lean on me to protect and honor them, that my clients and friends know that I will not accept people shrugging off their brilliance. Heck no! What about you? What makes you unique? Please share. The world needs more of that.
3. **Embrace your natural body shape.** We are built differently, so be the best kick-ass version of you. Instagram and the rest of the social media world is like the land of Oz––so much of it is a mirage. Put the fantasy of you where it belongs: in your heart. YOU know what is best for you, how to take better care of you, how to be a kinder person. The information to improve is right in front of you. Stop looking for it elsewhere. Love yourself, and stop seeking approval from the social media fantasy world. Put your phone down and go meet a friend, or call your mother, haha!
4. **Live with confidence from within.** Confidence is an inside job. I didn't win trophies necessarily because I always had the best body on stage. I often won because I was having

the most fun. I made a point to have a blast with the other competitors and to help others backstage, if needed. And I came prepared, because I knew if I didn't bring my A-game, it was not only disrespecting myself, but also the rest of the people at the event. Not playing an A-game was absolutely non-negotiable. Where in your life are you ready to play an A-game? Once you decide, it's time to take action. But first, you have to shift your mindset

5. **Embrace and reframe the fear.** Look at your fear as a doorway that will take you to a better version of you. We all have fears, both real and imagined. Forward motion that leads to positive changes in your life cannot exist without it. Identify the fear as a combination of fear and excitement, or any other word that fits for you, and continue to lean in.

For example, knowing that I was going to experience greater financial freedom through the success of my gold company, I still felt a tinge of fear mixed with the excitement as I knew relationships around me would be shifting in a big way. It's the same when I am approaching a fitness competition: what if I trip on stage in my high heels, my suit flies off, or any other crazy thing that passed through my mind while filled with wild excitement to compete and win.

Be clear on what you desire as the end result, and keep moving through— you will be so proud of yourself for pushing through to the other side. Self-esteem is rooted in the belief that you are here to do more, to be more. Trust in yourself enough to know that you deserve all you desire. You really do...

"It doesn't matter who you are, where you come from. The ability to triumph begins with you. Always." —Oprah Winfrey

Badass Body – The New YOU Starts Here

"Excellence in anything increases your potential in everything."
— Joe Rogan

Ask anyone in the coaching profession the same questions, and you will probably get the same two-word answer, "it depends" … No, we are not being cagey or mysterious.

It's just that we understand the multitude of variables that make up the best exercise and nutrition plan, business strategy, or relationship goals for each individual.

No, you certainly cannot transform your life overnight, but what you can do is transform it from today *for the rest of your life.* Once you experience the life-changing benefits, I can guarantee it will be a feeling you will never want to lose.

As a long-time fitness enthusiast, it is my firm belief that success in all areas of life is a result of pushing through the inertia that pushes back at us every day to stay in our comfort zones. And if you haven't yet received the memo, motivation to *be* more, to *do* more, does not happen in there. Ideas come and go— just one more pass at the fast food drive-through, "I'm just going to stay in this relationship because I'm comfortable", "I will start a new job search, write that book, begin to exercise tomorrow".

Sorry, but tomorrow is not a day of the week. Unless you get up and get moving, all of your goodness dies on the vine. One of my favorite quotes from motivational speaker Les Brown is this: "Where are the richest places in the world? Is it Dubai? Silicon

Valley? Wall Street? Nope. It's the cemetery, because that is where great ideas die with the people who failed to take action on them."

Please, don't let that be you.

The body is the machine that drives you through life, and so it is imperative that we start here on our transformation to ensure a greater success in all areas of our lives. Study after study shows that fitness and health is an indicator of quality of life. You can't get too far driving a piece of junk. Isn't it time you took the bull by the horns? Time you took the steps necessary to fuel yourself like a Ferrari?

Below are some basic principles and general guidelines to get you on your way to feeling fit and in flow in as little as four weeks. That's right! In four weeks, you can look and feel better than you have in years: more energy, more vitality, more flexibility, not to mention the positive internal shifts that occur when you commit to transform your body through exercise and clean nutrition.

Basic Nutritional Guidelines

Cleaning up your nutrition is the quickest way to level-up your overall well being, bar none. By combining a healthy diet with a weight training plan, you will be well on your way to experiencing greater vitality and weight loss. Check out these basic nutritional guidelines below:

1. **Consume high-quality protein at every meal.** Lean meats, like chicken and turkey, or fish are my staples. Protein is essential as you increase your exercise, so your body has enough muscle building protein to develop and maintain lean tissue, while at the same time losing fat. It is possible to go vegan and build muscle, but it is a total

commitment that very few people I know have attained. I am not saying it is impossible, it just takes a huge level of discipline. I have not eaten red meat since I was 15. I tried the vegan thing, but I feel most vibrant, strong, and alive when I keep my protein up to at least 3/4 grams per pound of body weight.

2. **Eat healthy fat!** Good-bye to the fat-free diets, which were just our foods loaded with extra sugar without the appetite-satisfying experience of fat. Add avocado or a small amount of nuts or seeds to your day, and notice your sugar cravings fade away. Your skin and all your cells will thank you!
3. **Go for the greens!** Load up on the lower starch veggies like broccoli, spinach, and asparagus. Eat your meals over a bed of greens to add an extra nutritional punch. Ramp up your greens slowly, as the added fiber can take the body a bit to adjust to.
4. **Avoid sugary and starchy foods!** A good clue is if you feel bloated and constipated after eating something, this is a pretty good sign that your body is not happy with what you are fueling it with. Complex starches, like three to four ounces of sweet potato or 1/3 cup of brown rice may be added to a meal to mix things up.
5. **Limit fruit and milk.** I generally get the biggest kick back from clients on this one. What I have seen with many clients is far too much fruit is being consumed on a daily basis, which converts to a simple sugar, only to be burned off quickly by the body, without adding the benefits of proteins and fats. Milk also causes bloating for people. Only after some of my clients have reduced or eliminated dairy have noticed a flatter tummy and less gastric upset. I suggest limiting fruit consumption to apples and berries for a couple

weeks, and take note of the changes you experience. I bet you will be pleasantly surprised, and delightfully less bloated.

Basic Exercise Plan Guidelines

The countless studies performed on exercise don't lie: lifting weights gives you an edge in so many areas of your life including: less belly fat, decreased risk of diabetes, decreased risk of heart disease, elevated mood, decreased anxiety and depression, and less pain in joints, not to mention the fact that your clothes will fit better, you will have increased energy, vitality, and an overall more positive outlook on life.

Here are some basic guidelines to weight training, based on the questions I am most frequently asked:

How many days a week should I lift? At least two, ideally three to four. Taking 48 hours off between workouts is at the long end of the metabolic boosting benefits of the weight training window. Doing a total body workout—one exercise per body part—is a great way to start the two times a week cycle. But please, take time to restore your body as well! Seven days a week of heavy lifting is overtraining, and will cause a definite back slide in meeting your goals. We all need restorative time. Take yours!

How much weight should I use? This is probably the most frequent question and the trickiest to answer. Oftentimes at the beginning, it's just trial and error. For people who have lifted a lot, this is second nature, but if you are a beginner, don't stress too much about it. Just grab a weight and go through the range of motion with the exercise. If you can perform 15 reps easily, then most likely, the weight is too light. Go up on the next set. The general rule is if you are shooting for ten reps, you should be feeling the weight and perhaps slowing down a bit through range of motion by rep seven or eight.

Trust in your body knowing what is right for it, but also do not be afraid to push the body so that you are uncomfortable. As in other areas of life, our greatest growth happens on the edges. Don't be afraid to go there.

How many repetitions should I do? This is a crucial question to ask yourself when you start a set. Why? Because it helps you set a goal for each set. Want to lose weight? Higher reps may be in order? Build shapelier muscles? Maybe a lower number of reps is required. Generally, I train clients in the 10 to 15 range; however, some clients do lower reps and heavier weight to shake up the workout or if a body part is lagging in strength compared to the body as a whole. Weight training is a dance. Understand that no work-out will ever be the same, because there are so many variables that come into play: energy level, fuel in the body, muscle soreness, injury, lack of focus, time of day—any of these can affect your workout. Just stay focused, and don't give up, no matter if you feel like it or not. You will not regret it.

How long should I rest between sets? Well, with my clients, they pay me for a killer workout, and I make sure they get their money's worth! However, generally one-minute rest between sets is ample, especially if you are mixing up body parts. For example, doing back and chest or biceps and triceps together.

Go to the gym prepared to work with your work-out set. When you step into the gym, be clear on your goals. Efficiency is key. Don't be distracted by idle conversation or sidetracked by others. Your time at the gym is precious. It's time to make your health and wellness goals #1.

It is truly possible to experience a body transformation in less than four weeks. By combining a high protein-lower carb diet, with an efficient weight training program, you are creating the most effective formula for shedding fat, building muscle, and quickly improving your health and wellbeing. You will never regret a day of improved health.

5 Common Mistakes People Make that Gets in the Way of Becoming a Badass

"The greatest mistake you can make in life is to be continually fearing you will make one." — Elbert Hubbard

Feeling stuck meeting your health and wellness goals? Discouraged by your lack of gains in your overall fitness level? Having a hard time tapping into your positivity mojo and lacking the confidence to follow through? You are not alone. Achieving any form of transformation takes not just motivation, but a well thought out strategy to ensure your success in becoming a badass.

Check out these five mistakes so many of us make when we embark on getting healthier all around. By avoiding these pitfalls, you will be over the rumble strip and back on the freeway of health and confident in no time. Follow the tips below to overcome your personal roadblocks. I know you want it. You wouldn't have read this far if you didn't. Let me help you find your way to your best self.

1. **Setting unrealistic goals**. Dream big, but take in consideration what is biologically possible for a human being. Lose ten pounds in a week, get completely buff in a month. Be free of self-sabotaging behaviors that shortchange your success. To be fit and healthy, start by viewing the journey as more of a marathon than a sprint. And as the saying goes, Rome was not built in a day. Start with one intentional step, and build from there.

Give yourself a realistic, but challenging goal: one that really excites you, so you will keep at it and be fired up to attain it. Set a big, audacious goal, then, break it down into bite-size chunks. Then, put your head down and pursue it like you mean it, even when you do not feel like it! This is how successful people attain their goals. They push right on through the "I don't feel like it" and, then, bask in their success on the other side. You can do that, too. You just have to want it bad enough. Life provides so many distractions. This is why it is so important to be clear on your goals and the vision of how it will look and feel when you achieve a fit positive lifestyle. You got this.

2. **Not eating breakfast**. It's called "breaking-a fast" for a reason. Your body has not had nutrition for hours after waking up. Be kind to your temple and refuel. Your body craves a healthy protein and a complex carb to fuel you through your day, not coffee and a donut. Adopt the high-test fuel rule in the morning with clean food that will jump start your day. I know there are people out there who don't agree with me on this one, but I have to say that through my extensive experience in the fitness field, the people who have the greatest long-term weight loss success, are those who fuel themselves with clean foods on a regular *and* consistent basis. Starving yourself between meals can often result in bingeing, and unfortunately, not always on the food your body needs to be healthy. Eat consistent. Eat clean. Keep the water up. This is the ticket to getting the lean and mean body you desire.
3. **Drinking alcohol**. Our culture is saturated with alcohol consumption that infiltrates all areas of our lives. In fact, many colleges are breeding grounds for alcohol abuse. "Alcoholism is the third leading lifestyle-related cause of

death in the United States, coming after tobacco and unhealthy diets and/or lack of exercise. A person who succumbs to excessive alcohol use loses a potential of 30 years of potential life, and as many as 40 percent of all the hospital beds across the country are used to treat health conditions that develop from alcoholism." (www.alcohol.org)

Why do I bring this up? Because our body's ability to process excess consumption is limited and will cause issues as a result. A lot of people use the excuse, "I only do it on the weekend" or "I just drink wine/vodka/beer, what is so bad about that?". Alcohol in excessive amounts wreaks havoc on your fitness and wellness goals. Don't set yourself back by obliterating your gains with excessive alcohol. Your body will thank you. Your emotional state will thank you. Self-respect means honoring the body you have; booze binging is simply just not that. You deserve better.

4. **Not staying hydrated**. I know, I know, I hear it all the time that drinking water is a total pain in the neck. But it is a habit that is crucial as part of your health and wellness goals. Your body tissues love the flush, including your skin. The optimal amount is no less than 50 percent of your body weight in ounces of water. Initially, you may feel bloated; however, your body does adjust to the extra fluid. Soon, you will notice a healthier glow to your skin, a flatter belly, and even less fatigue and mood swings. Studies have shown that often drinking more water increases energy and alertness. Some tips to get more water in? Infuse your water with lemon, lime, or cucumber and mint. Drinking water at room temperature is easier for some to drink. Mark a container with check marks based on times of day, or use an

app on your phone as a reminder. Drink non-caffeinated tea. Bottoms up!

5. **Not getting enough sleep**. The truth is when we don't get enough sleep, we are less likely to stay committed to our fitness and wellness goals, make poor choices with food, drink less water, and have an increased chance of injury. Don't let that be you! Commit to going to bed close to the same time every night, be sure to get adequate exercise every day (a minimum of 30 minutes daily exercise is recommended), and be careful not to drink alcohol too close to bedtime, which can disturb your sleep. Turn off your phone— leave it out of your room if you have to— to ensure a good night's sleep.

By avoiding these common mistakes, you will experience greater vitality, increased feel-good hormones, and a healthier physique. You deserve to live an amazing life! Take small steps daily to live positively fit, and watch your overall happiness and pleasure in life elevate. It is your time.

Workbook #18:

1. What changes are you ready to take on to live a healthier lifestyle?

____

____

____

____

____

2. What habits do you have that you know are negatively affecting your life? Are you ready to admit them to yourself, and to get the help and support you need to be the best version of you?

---

3. Success starts with small increments of change: what are you ready to say "yes" to, to have a more fulfilling life?

Mindfulness Over Matter: Helpful Tips to Mind your Stress and Eat Well

"You cannot always control what goes on outside. But you can always control what goes on inside." — *Wayne Dyer*

There has been a large focus in the media about mindfulness and how important this is to create a healthier and more balanced lifestyle. There has been a wealth of information on meditation, mindful breathing, mindful exercise— like yoga and tai chi, and even mindful eating.

I appreciate the value of these studies, and apply these principles to my life on a daily basis. It really works! And then... life happens! And the problem is— particularly when we are talking about mindful eating— that most of us are not living in a monastery or an igloo, and the stress of everyday life is real and oftentimes unavoidable.

It's not like we can stop everything and sit and meditate when it's five o'clock and your kids are cranky and starving, or you have ten things to do before you leave the house and the cat just threw up on your rug, or how about that S.O.S. call from your friend, when you are already feeling tapped out and overwhelmed?

Can you relate? I know I certainly can.

In our current multi-tasking culture, how can we truly take the "mind" out of the equation and create an environment that supports healthy food habits and choices? Because the truth is this:

eating well is 70 percent of the getting fit game when we are talking about up-leveling our overall health and wellness.

And this being the case, how do we create an environment that encourages healthy eating and makes the process actually more, shall we say, mindless, than mindful? In other words, setting our life so we are less distracted by cupcakes and chips and more focused on making healthy choices.

Is it possible?

Absolutely.

Let's review some quick tips for you to apply immediately:

But first, we must embrace that the ticket to success is that preparation is always our best offense!

Nothing blows a diet faster than not being prepared when the tornado called life sweeps in. View the whole concept of preparation as a habit you develop, always fine-tuning your process along the way. It doesn't have to be perfect, just focus on getting better on a daily basis.

Here are some areas where we can streamline our process that are solution-based, so you too can get your fit on:

1. When cooking, always create a few extra meals out of what you are making. Package them up for a quick grab-and-go. Never make just one meal when it takes the same amount of effort to make four!

2. Keep fresh fruits and vegetables in the middle of your fridge at eye level. NO cases of soda in the fridge; try to keep a few different seltzer flavors easily accessible so you can grab one when you have

a soda craving. Hard boiled eggs are a great protein snack. Make living healthy easy on you by making the inside of your fridge reflect the inner you- abundant and healthy!

3. Keep all the less-than-healthy snacks in a separate drawer and definitely not in plain sight. What you see, you will chew, so either put them up high or even in a drawer with a "childproof" lock. Any time that you can build a pause in before you grab the snack will be a moment where you can assess your true hunger and recheck your resolve.

4. Keep your counters clear of snack foods. Studies were performed with participants, and they assessed their counters and determined that cereal and chips were huge culprits in weakening your resolve on your food choices. What the study found is that people who had just fruit on their counter were the slimmest of the bunch. How does your counter look? Take a moment to make a sweep of your counter areas and make the changes necessary to clear away the unhealthy food clutter.

5. When going out to eat, order a side of vegetables as an appetizer. This was my go-to strategy when my kids were small. I always got a good chuckle when the server came back to the table after my kids inhaled their huge bowl of broccoli in no time. It worked, and they still love their veggies!

6. Put a lid on it. You are less likely to eat more candy or any other food if there is a cover on it. If you are committed to eating family style at the table, always put covers on the food. Make a salad the one bowl that always comes full and fresh to the table for your family. This is a great habit, and one that will last a lifetime. When I was a kid, when we ordered pizza for take-out, we had to also eat a salad, and I still do.

7. Hit the grocery store with a list and a strategy. The middle aisles of the store are where the more processed foods lie, so shop the periphery for the freshest goods. Grocery cart always looking the same? That is not a bad sign. That's what herbs and spices are for. And if you do get a treat food, be sure it goes right to the highest shelf in your kitchen or a less accessible area. One of my friends always puts her ice cream in the downstairs fridge, so she will have to walk down the stairs if she really wants that bowl.

8. Eat off smaller plates and use smaller bowls for your meals. Fill your plate with veggies and proteins and savor the flavors of simple and fresh foods. Make a big batch of protein rich soup with any leftovers a couple days a week. Yum!

9. Make eating healthier more convenient for yourself. Streamline your habits and the way you set up your home and work, so you are less tempted by junk and more stimulated to move. Chaos in your outside environment breeds chaos in your internal environment. Cut yourself some slack. Clean it up, let go of the stuff that drags you down. Make way for healthier ways of experiencing the good that surrounds you. You are worth it.

10. Be kinder and gentler to yourself by taking control of your relationships and let go of thoughts and feelings that cause you distress. Sometimes, this may include creating a healthy distance with some people in your life. Don't feel guilty about creating healthy boundaries with people. If you are clear on your goals, making healthier choices in all areas of your life are just easier. Are you clear? If not, what will it take to get there?

You deserve to be healthy. You deserve to have a higher level of peace in your life, free of negative self-talk and chaotic thinking. By creating a system of success, you will be well on your way to being the fit and fabulous badass you came here to be.

IGNITE YOUR HAPPINESS THROUGH EXERCISE

Warning: Exercise has been known to cause health and happiness!

What does a perfect day look like to you? What are you doing? Who are you with? And does some form of exercise fall into that perfect day?

If not, you are not alone.

A recent study put out by BMC Public Health highlights a fascinating revelation: it is not lack of time or other excuses non-exercisers use that prohibit so many from exercising; but actually, their own beliefs about putting themselves first in their own self-care that derails them. In other words, we feel that if we add exercise into our day, it will take away from other must-do's in our lives, like taking care of others. Many view taking time to exercise as selfish or decadent.

The BMC study referenced above used two different focus groups classified as low and high "actives" and interviewed them about their thoughts and experiences with exercise as well as what made them feel happy and successful. What did their perfect day look like, and why?

Their top four feel-goods in the participants in the study were as follows:

1. Connecting with others.
2. Being of service to others.

3. Participating in leisure activities and hobbies.
4. Feeling relaxed and free from daily pressure.

Do these four resonate with you?

What I found most interesting about this study was that the "low active" group viewed exercise as hindering their ability of those happiness indicators listed above; whereas, the "high active" group placed exercise as integral to their internal happiness quotient.

Why the difference?

What the study highlights is that we may be looking at exercise, and what motivates and drives us to take part, from the wrong vantage point. The question now becomes: in what way can we inspire the "low active" group to shift their belief from thinking exercise takes away their happy, to now believing that exercise actually enhances the four feel-goods listed above.

Much of my work as a coach is doing just that. Helping people in the "low active" group to gradually shift their beliefs. That instead of exercise taking away their experience of happiness and success, it is actually enhancing it.

Let's go over some strategies— what I like to call mind-shifting— that will help you do just that.

1. Start to imagine that exercise will actually bring you closer to others, not draw you away. People who choose an active lifestyle very often find a community of like-minded individuals who support each other through their fitness process. Nothing is more motivating to not only be inspired, but also inspire others on your wellness journey. It's such an immediate feel good. Some suggestions include: taking a

walk with your partner, riding bikes with your kids, making new friends at the gym, and trying a yoga class.

This is actually one of the primary reasons I love my work as a coach so much. The relationships I build with my clients add such a rich quality to my life, I cannot imagine *not* doing it! Trust that adding fitness into your life will enhance your relations with others. Vitality is a wonderful quality to share.

2. Do you feel you don't have time to work out because you are too busy caring for others? Well, I have to ask you, how well are you able to care for others if you feel sick, tired, fatigued, and put-upon day in and day out? It's time to stop this self-limiting and unhealthy belief. Now is the perfect time to adopt a new way of self-talk that promotes your taking better care of YOU. There is nothing noble about sacrificing your own health by putting others' well-being in front of your own. It's time for you to start declaring that out loud. You deserve to be healthy. You really do. Please claim this once and for all.
3. Find a form of exercise that lights you up. Some people just love Zumba. For others, it's hot yoga, lifting weights, or hiking in the woods. Give yourself permission to go for it. The afterglow of post exercise, both physically and emotionally, is REAL and can last for hours, even days. It's your turn to participate in your life. Not only will you sleep better, but will also likely experience a significant decrease in pain and inflammation, not to mention the added benefit of lower incidences of anxiety and depression. Belly dancing anyone?

Each day is a gift. It is up to us on how we want to design it. Give yourself permission to set an intention on what your best day will look like. Imagine yourself as your happiest, healthiest, and most badass self. As the expression goes, we reap what we sow. Isn't it time you sowed the seeds of your highest and best self?

I am here, cheering you on!

Kate McKay

ABOUT THE AUTHOR

Kate McKay is living proof that every single one of us is capable of overcoming adversity and living the most amazing life they can imagine. Even despite experiencing the worst tragedy of a parent, the loss of her son in 2017, Kate continues to be a positive force of inspiration for others; she is deeply committed to helping others overcome adversity by providing actionable tools to live a breakthrough life.

Growing up as one of nine children in a suburb of Boston, Kate struggled early on with feelings of self-doubt and negative self-worth. Often feeling out of place in both her family and school, Kate continued to strive to be more, to do more and really hit her stride when she walked through the doors of Walnut Hill School of the Performing Arts in Natick, MA. Here Kate found her passion in the class that Kate proclaims was the only thing she ever got A's in-Theater.

Kate continued her study in Theater at Bennington College and found her deeper passion for fitness and wellness here. In fact, Kate believes that this passion for health is what helped her get through the tragic loss of her brother to murder when she was 23.

Living enthusiastically has always been Kate's M.O; her hunger for knowledge and desire to share what she learns to help others to be their best has always been her driving force in life. Being a mom was a natural extension of this and Kate embraced this role with her three children wholeheartedly.

At age 41, however, Kate found herself overweight, out of shape and deeply despondent. She felt stuck in a financially strapped and unhappy marriage. Her lack of confidence hit an all-time low. One day, after dragging herself to the gym, she looked in the mirror and realized that no one was going to rescue her from her mess but her. She committed to re-write her story and reclaim her life, so with the support of a couple great coaches, she did just that.

McKay accepted this personal mission to get into the best shape of her life, at 43, she entered and won her first bikini competition. Kate continued to compete in several competitions through the age of 54. In addition, to conquer her scarcity mentality and to create a financially stable home for her children and her own future, Kate started and built a multi-million dollar business out of her home, even though she had never taken a single business class in her life.

In 2017, tragedy struck Kate's life once again with the suicide of her son Will. As painful as this was, Kate realized that she needed to use her public influence as an author, speaker and coach to be a messenger of healing and growth for others. In fact, this loss has instilled a faith and confidence in her purpose and passion that fuels her every day to be a conduit of hope and strength for others. Kate believes this is her legacy and lives in this clarity in her every waking hour.

McKay's desire to inspire and motivate others has resulted in her continued growth of her consulting and coaching practice, helping others build an amazing life from the inside out by providing actionable tools to aid in deepening our own personal awareness so to heal our wounds and embrace being a badass in every area of our lives.

With her direct but extremely nurturing approach, McKay encourages others to live happier and more fulfilling lives with a clear sense of purpose, infused with a resilient and playful spirit.

Kate is the author of Living Sexy Fit at Any Age, contributes monthly as a columnist in the Newburyport Daily News, has written for Entrepreneur, appeared in numerous national and local radio, podcasts and tv, including PBS. Kate has been interviewed and appeared in several magazines and newspaper articles.

Kate grew up in Massachusetts and still resides there in a seaside community of Newburyport.

How Can You Help?

Thank You for Reading My Book!

I really appreciate all of your feedback, and I love hearing what you have to say.

I need your input to make the next version of this book and my future books better.

Please leave me an honest review on Amazon letting me know what you thought of the book.

Thanks so much!

Kate McKay

The Breakthrough Catalyst

HOW TO WORK WITH KATE MCKAY, THE BREAKTHROUGH CATALYST!

Want more information on how you can hire Kate to Speak at your event or work with her one-one as your Coach?

Click here: Work With Kate

Visit Kate's website: www.kate-mckay.com

Follow Kate McKay:

Facebook: https://www.facebook.com/TheBreakthroughCatalyst

Twitter: https://twitter.com/Katemckay18

Linked In: https://www.linkedin.com/in/kate-mckay-b10a462a/

Instagram @KateMcKayCoach

Made in the USA
Monee, IL
05 May 2020

29182988R00085